JN086670

Amazing Space
Black Holes, Planets, Rockets, and More

by Ed Jacob

Level 5

IBC パブリッシング

はじめに

　ラダーシリーズは、「はしご (ladder)」を使って一歩一歩上を目指すように、学習者の実力に合わせ、無理なくステップアップできるよう開発された英文リーダーのシリーズです。

　リーディング力をつけるためには、繰り返したくさん読むこと、いわゆる「多読」がもっとも効果的な学習法であると言われています。多読では、「1. 速く 2. 訳さず英語のまま 3. なるべく辞書を使わず」に読むことが大切です。スピードを計るなど、速く読むよう心がけましょう（たとえば TOEIC® テストの音声スピードはおよそ 1 分間に 150 語です）。そして 1 語ずつ訳すのではなく、英語を英語のまま理解するくせをつけるようにします。こうして読み続けるうちに語感がついてきて、だんだんと英語が理解できるようになるのです。まずは、ラダーシリーズの中からあなたのレベルに合った本を選び、少しずつ英文に慣れ親しんでください。たくさんの本を手にとるうちに、英文書がすらすら読めるようになってくるはずです。

《本シリーズの特徴》

- 中学校レベルから中級者レベルまで5段階に分かれています。自分に合ったレベルからスタートしてください。
- クラシックから現代文学、ノンフィクション、ビジネスと幅広いジャンルを扱っています。あなたの興味に合わせてタイトルを選べます。
- 巻末のワードリストで、いつでもどこでも単語の意味を確認できます。レベル1、2では、文中の全ての単語が、レベル3以上は中学校レベル外の単語が掲載されています。
- カバーにヘッドホーンマークのついているタイトルは、オーディオ・サポートがあります。ウェブから購入／ダウンロードし、リスニング教材としても併用できます。

《使用語彙について》

レベル1：中学校で学習する単語約1000語

レベル2：レベル1の単語＋使用頻度の高い単語約300語

レベル3：レベル1の単語＋使用頻度の高い単語約600語

レベル4：レベル1の単語＋使用頻度の高い単語約1000語

レベル5：語彙制限なし

Contents

【本書に出てくる主な関連用語】

英語は、科学の分野で最も一般的な言語の一つです。特に、宇宙に興味がある人にとっては、英語は欠かせません。英語で宇宙を学ぶことで、世界中の人々と科学的な知識を共有し、国際的なコミュニケーションの能力を高めることができます。この本では、宇宙に関する様々なトピックを英語で紹介しています。本文中に出てくる用語についてあらかじめ日本語で確認して、基本的な知識を身につけておきましょう。

アルテミス計画	Artemis program	アメリカ合衆国連邦政府が出資する有人宇宙飛行（月面着陸）計画
イトカワ	Itokawa	太陽系の小惑星であり、地球に接近する地球近傍小惑星のうちアポロ群に属する
インジェニュイティ	Ingenuity	NASAのマーズ2020ミッションの一環として火星で運用されている小型のロボットヘリコプター
衛星攻撃兵器	anti-satellite weapons (ASATs)	地球周回軌道上の人工衛星を攻撃する兵器
エウロパ	Europa	木星の第2衛星。月よりわずかに小さく、太陽系内の衛星の中では6番目に大きい
エリス	Eris	冥王星型天体の1つに属する準惑星
オポチュニティ	Opportunity	NASAの火星探査車で、マーズ・エクスプロレーション・ローバー計画で使用された2台の探査車のうちの2号機
オリオン	Orion	NASAがスペースシャトルの代替として開発中の有人ミッション用の宇宙船
オリオン腕	Orion Arm	銀河系の比較的小規模な渦状腕の1つであり、現時点で太陽系が通過中の渦状腕

カイパーベルト	Kuiper Belt	太陽系の海王星軌道より外側からにある、天体が密集した穴の空いた円盤状の領域であり、星周円盤の一種
カッシーニ	Cassini	NASAと欧州宇宙機関 (ESA) によって開発され、1997年に打上げられた土星探査機
ガニメデ	Ganymede	木星の第3衛星。太陽系に存在する衛星の中で半径、質量ともに最大
ガリレオ	Galileo	1989年10月18日にNASAが打ち上げた木星探査機
カロン	Charon	冥王星の第1衛星かつ冥王星最大の衛星
軌道ロケットブースター	orbital rocket booster	多段式の打ち上げロケットの最初の段階、または持続ロケットと並行して使用される短時間燃焼するロケット
キュリオシティ	Curiosity	NASAが火星探査ミッションで用いる無人探査車
銀河団	galaxy cluster	数百個から数千個の銀河が互いの重力の影響によって集団となったもの
クエーサー	quasar	非常に離れた距離に存在し極めて明るく輝いているために、恒星のような点光源に見える天体
ケスラーシンドローム	Kessler syndrome	スペースデブリの危険性を端的に説明するシミュレーションモデル。
ケレス	Ceres	火星と木星の間の小惑星帯 (メインベルト) に位置する準惑星
国際宇宙ステーション	International Space Station (ISS)	低軌道にあるモジュール式の宇宙ステーション。科学研究を行う微小重力と宇宙環境の研究所として機能
ゴルディロックス・ゾーン	Goldilocks zone	宇宙において生命の進化に適した領域のこと
指向性エネルギー兵器	directed-energy weapons (DEWs)	目標に対し指向性のエネルギーを直接に照射攻撃を行い、目標物を破壊したり機能を停止させる兵器

祝融号	Zhurong	マーズ・ローバーであり、中国が最初に地球以外の惑星に上陸させた探査車
ジュノー	Juno	2011年8月5日に打ち上げられたNASAの木星探査機。2016年7月5日に木星の極軌道への投入に成功
準惑星	dwarf planet	太陽の周囲を公転する惑星以外の天体のうち、それ自身の重力によって球形になれる質量を有するもの
小惑星帯	asteroid belt	小惑星が密集している火星軌道と木星軌道の間の領域
スーパーアース	super Earth	太陽系外惑星のうち地球の数倍の質量を持ち、かつ主成分が岩石や金属などの固体成分と推定された惑星
スターリンク	Starlink	アメリカ合衆国の民間企業スペースXが運用している衛星インターネットアクセスサービス
スペースデブリ	space debris	地球を周回する人工衛星・打ち上げロケットの残骸
静止軌道	geostationary orbit (GEO)	地球の自転周期と衛星の公転周期が一致している軌道。地上からは常に静止しているように見える
星団	star cluster	同じガスから誕生した、互いの重力相互作用によって結びついた恒星の集団
タイタン	Titan	土星の第6衛星で最大の衛星
地球低軌道	low Earth Orbit (LEO)	地球の周囲を周回する軌道で、周期が128分以下（1日に少なくとも11.25周する）の軌道
中性子星	neutron star	大質量星が超新星爆発を起こした後に残る、ほぼ中性子だけで構成された超高密度の天体
超新星	supernova	大質量の恒星や近接連星系の白色矮星が起こす大規模な爆発（超新星爆発）によって輝く天体のこと

電磁放射線	electromagnetic radiation	放射線のうち電磁波であるものをいい、一般に、赤外線、可視光線、紫外線、エックス線、ガンマ線をさす
天問1号	Tianwen-1	中華人民共和国が2020年7月23日に打ち上げに成功した火星探査ミッションで用いる探査機の名称
特異点	singularity	宇宙が膨らむ前に存在した無限に小さな点
トリトン	Triton	海王星最大の衛星で、海王星で発見された初めての衛星
ニュー・ホライズンズ	New Horizons	2006年に打ち上げた、人類初の冥王星を含む太陽系外縁天体の探査を行うための無人探査機
ネオワイズ彗星	Comet NEOWISE	赤外線観測衛星NEOWISEによって2020年に発見された長周期彗星
パーサヴィアランス	Perseverance	NASAのマーズ2020ミッションの一環として、火星のジェゼロクレーターを探査するためのマーズ・ローバー
バイキング1号	Viking 1	NASAのバイキング計画で火星に送られた2機の探査機のうち最初の1機
バイキング2号	Viking 2	火星探査計画であるバイキング計画の一部で、バイキング1号に続くもの
ハウメア	Haumea	準惑星であり、太陽系外縁天体のサブグループである冥王星型天体の1つ
パスファインダー	Pathfinder	NASA・JPLがディスカバリー計画の一環として行った火星探査計画、またはその探査群の総称
ハッブル宇宙望遠鏡	Hubble Space Telescope (HST)	1990年4月24日に打ち上げられた、地上約600km上空の軌道上を周回する宇宙望遠鏡
はやぶさ	Hayabusa	2003年5月9日に宇宙科学研究所(ISAS)が打ち上げた小惑星探査機

ハレー彗星	Halley's Comet	75.32年周期で地球に接近する短周期彗星。多くの周期彗星の中で最初に知られた彗星
微惑星	planetesimal	太陽系の形成初期に存在したと考えられている微小天体
ブラックホール	black hole	極めて高密度で、極端に重力が強いために物質だけでなく光さえ脱出することができない天体
プロキシマ・ケンタウリ	Proxima Centauri	ケンタウルス座の方向に4.246光年離れた位置にある赤色矮星。太陽系に最も近い恒星として知られている
ボイジャー2号	Voyager 2	NASAにより1977年8月20日に打ち上げられた、木星よりも遠くの外惑星及び衛星の探査を目的として開発・運用されている無人宇宙探査機
ホット・ジュピター	hot Jupiter	木星ほどの質量を持つガス惑星でありながら、主星の恒星からわずかしか離れておらず、表面温度が非常に高温になっている太陽系外惑星の分類の一つ
マーズ・ローバー	Mars rover	火星着陸後に火星表面を自動で走行するローバー
マケマケ	Makemake	準惑星であり、太陽系外縁天体のサブグループである冥王星型天体の1つ
マゼラン	Magellan	NASAが1989年に打ち上げた惑星探査機。金星を探査してレーダーにより金星地表の地形を明らかにした
マゼラン雲	Magellanic Clouds	銀河系の近くにある2つの銀河、大マゼラン雲と小マゼラン雲の総称
ミランダ	Miranda	天王星の第5衛星。太陽系の中で最も極端かつ多様な地形を持つ
ロケット方程式	rocket equation	1897年にコンスタンチン・ツィオルコフスキーによって示されたロケット推進に関する公式

Introduction

Just 600 years ago, most of our world was unexplored and unknown. People in Europe knew little or nothing about the Americas, Africa, and large sections of Asia. However, during the Age of Discovery, between the fifteenth and seventeenth centuries, brave explorers set out in fragile wooden ships, attempting to cross entire oceans. During this period, maps of the world were quickly filled in, and human knowledge grew at an incredible speed as new places, animals, plants, and civilizations were discovered.

Today, we are beginning a new era, an age of exploration like the one that captured the hearts and minds of Europeans in the 1400s. But our destination is not the distant shores of a new continent; it is outer space. Our vessels are not sailing ships; they are powerful rockets.

And our quest is not merely to discover new lands but to unlock the secrets of the universe itself.

Just as the explorers of old attempted to expand their knowledge of the world, we, too, are driven by a thirst for knowledge. Our journey into the cosmos is not merely an adventure; it is a quest to find answers to questions about the origins of our planet, the nature of our existence, and the potential for life beyond the Earth.

Modern life depends on technology like satellites and on innovations and materials that were developed as a result of space exploration. During the Age of Exploration, the world that the explorers had opened up became increasingly important to Europeans, and so knowledge of our solar system and even the galaxies beyond it are likely to become more important to people on Earth in the near future.

Knowledge of space is no longer just a hobby for people who love science fiction or a specialized field of study for a few scientists. It is becoming an important part of our everyday lives that everyone in the world needs to have at least a basic understanding of.

Why, you might ask, is this new age of exploration so important? The answer lies in the power of knowledge. The discoveries we make in space have the potential to revolutionize our understanding of science, reshape our technology, and drive our economies to new heights.

Rockets have led to advancements in physics, engineering, and materials science. The knowledge gained from building and launching them has not only taken us to the moon and beyond but has also given birth to countless innovations that touch our everyday lives. From satellite technology that powers global communications to the development of high-tech materials used in medical devices, space exploration has a huge impact on our society.

As we set off on this cosmic voyage, we must remember that it is not just scientists and engineers who hold the key to our future in space. It is a journey that belongs to all of humanity, a collective effort to expand our horizons and knowledge. Just as the Age of Exploration brought people together across continents, our age of space exploration unites us across borders and cultures.

Part 1
Our Incredible Universe

第1部 私たちの驚異的な宇宙

　宇宙はビッグバンという驚異的な出来事から始まりました。空間が急速に膨張することで生み出されたエネルギーは、やがて物質の基本となる粒子に変わりました。最初の元素は水素やヘリウムでした。これらが結合していくことで、銀河や星、惑星などが作られていきました。

【主な用語や表現】

ページ
9	singularity	特異点
	particle	粒子
	building block	（物質の）構成要素 [単位], 成分
10	fusion	融合
11	white dwarf	白色矮星
	supernova	超新星
14	spiral galaxy	渦巻銀河
	elliptical galaxy	楕円銀河
	star cluster	星団
15	galaxy cluster	銀河団
	gravitational	重力の, 引力の
18	celestial	天の, 空の, 天体の
19	Ursa Major	おおぐま座
	Cygnus	白鳥座
	nebulae	nebula（星雲）の複数形
	grandeur	壮大さ, 雄大さ
20	supermassive	超大質量の
22	Magellanic Clouds	マゼラン雲
	orbit	軌道に乗る
23	furnace	炉, かまど, 溶鉱炉
	nuclear fusion	核融合
24	red giant	赤色巨星
	neutron star	中性子星
	city-sized	都市サイズ（数キロメートル程度）の
26	exoplanet	太陽系外惑星, 系外惑星
28	interstellar	星間の

The Birth of the Universe

In the beginning, there were no galaxies, no stars, and no planets. There was nothing but emptiness. The only thing that existed was a tiny, super-dense point. It was unimaginably small, but it also had an incredible amount of energy in it. This point, known as a singularity, is believed to be the origin of our universe.

Suddenly, a powerful burst of energy erupted from the singularity. This event, called the Big Bang, marked the beginning of our universe. It was like an enormous explosion, but instead of things being blown apart, space itself started expanding. Picture blowing up a balloon—as it inflates, everything on its surface moves farther away from everything else.

As space expanded, it carried energy with it. This energy transformed into particles, the building blocks of matter. Simple elements like hydrogen and helium formed during the early moments of the universe. These elements would eventually come together to create galaxies, stars, and planets.

In those early times, the universe was incredibly hot and dense. Temperatures were unimaginably high, reaching billions of degrees. As the universe expanded, it began to cool down, allowing particles to come together and form atoms. These atoms gathered to create clouds of gas.

Under the force of gravity, these gas clouds began to collapse in on themselves. As they contracted, they heated up and started to glow. In this way, the first stars were born. These were not like the stars we see in the night sky now—they were massive and blazing, radiating intense light and heat.

Inside these stars, an amazing process was taking place. Hydrogen atoms were fusing together to form helium. This fusion released an enormous amount of energy in the form of light and heat. It was like a cosmic furnace, turning simple elements into more complex ones.

But those stars couldn't shine forever. As they used up their nuclear fuel, they changed. Smaller stars would gradually cool down and shrink, becoming what we call white dwarfs.

Larger stars, on the other hand, would end their lives in a fiery explosion known as a supernova. These explosions were so powerful that they

Supernova (bright spot on the lower left)

scattered newly formed elements into space.

These elements became the building blocks for new stars, planets, and even us. Our bodies are made up of these elements—the carbon, oxygen, and other atoms that were created inside those ancient stars. It's a connection that ties us to the distant past of the universe.

The expansion of the universe is driven by a mysterious force called dark energy that no one has been able to measure so far. This force is causing galaxies to move away from each other at an accelerating rate. Imagine dots on a balloon's surface moving away from each other as you inflate it—that's how galaxies are spreading out in space.

While the universe is expanding, galaxies are also interacting with each other. Sometimes, galaxies collide and merge, creating new shapes and structures. Our Milky Way, for example, will collide with the Andromeda galaxy in the far future, billions of years from now.

So, the universe that began as a tiny, unimaginably hot and dense point has evolved into the vast and complex cosmos we see today. It's a story of incredible forces—gravity pulling things together, dark energy pushing them apart, and the powerful processes inside stars shaping everything around us. As we look up at the night sky, we're not just seeing stars; we're gazing at the ancient history of the universe itself.

Space Fact: The early universe was a very dark place! It was so dense that light could not travel freely. It took about 380,000 years for the universe to become transparent enough for light to travel easily through it.

Galaxies

In the vast darkness of space, there are giant collections of stars, gas, and dust known as galaxies. These galaxies come

Spiral Galaxy

in many shapes and sizes, and they hold countless mysteries.

Galaxies come in three main shapes: spiral, elliptical, and irregular. Think of a spiral galaxy as a spinning pinwheel with arms that stretch outward. Our own Milky Way is a spiral galaxy. Elliptical galaxies, on the other hand, are like round or oval blobs of stars. Irregular galaxies have a more random and scattered appearance.

Scientists have looked into space using powerful telescopes to study galaxies. They've found out that galaxies are like families of stars, living together in the same cosmic neighborhood. These stars are born, live their lives, and sometimes even explode in bursts called supernovae. Galaxies also have neighborhoods within them, called star clusters. These are groups of stars that are close neighbors and often share a common origin.

Galaxies are not just full of stars. They also

contain clouds of gas and tiny bits of dust. These clouds are like space nurseries where new stars are born. Gravity pulls the gas and dust together, and over time, they form into stars.

One important thing scientists have learned is that galaxies are not just scattered randomly in space. Instead, they gather together in groups

Galaxy Cluster Abell 2744

called galaxy clusters. These are like cities of galaxies, all held together by gravity. Just as people come together in cities, galaxies gather in clusters, attracting each other with their gravitational pull.

Now, let's think about numbers for a moment. The size of galaxies is measured in light-years. A light-year is the distance that light travels in one year, and light is really fast.

It moves at 299,792,458 meters per second, and it can go around the Earth about seven times in just one second! A typical galaxy is about 30,000 light years across, and galaxies can be incredibly far apart. The nearest galaxy to our Milky Way is called the Andromeda galaxy. It's about 2.5 million light-years away from us.

As we look up at the night sky, we're not just seeing stars but entire galaxies, each with its own stories and mysteries. Galaxies are like the building blocks of the universe, forming its structure and beauty. Stay curious and keep looking up at the stars—they're the key to unlocking the secrets of our universe.

Space Fact: The largest known galaxy in the universe is IC 1101, which is about 50 times the size of the Milky Way. It has a diameter of about 6 million light-years and contains about 100 trillion stars. It is located about 1.07 billion light-years away from us.

The Milky Way Galaxy

Imagine looking up at the night sky, and among the stars, you find a glowing band stretching across the darkness. That bright band is our home in the universe—the Milky Way galaxy. Let's uncover some fascinating facts about this vast cosmic neighborhood.

The Milky Way is like a giant city of stars, gas, and dust, and it's the place where we live. It's so big that if you could somehow travel at the speed of light it would take you about 100,000 years to go from one end to the other.

The Milky Way Galaxy

Speaking of speed, the Milky Way is spinning incredibly fast. It moves around at 210 kilometers per second! Imagine if you could watch the Milky Way from above. You would see that it is moving like the hands of a giant clock. Although it is amazingly fast moving, it takes around 250 million years for our galaxy to complete a single spin. That's much longer than dinosaurs lived on the Earth!

Our Sun is just one of the many stars swirling around in the Milky Way. Think of stars as the city lights, and we're like a tiny glow among them. We're located about halfway from the center of the Milky Way to its edge. This place is called the Orion Arm, and it's like a cozy suburb of our galactic city.

The Milky Way has a family of stars known as constellations. These are groups of stars that people long ago imagined as shapes of animals, objects, and heroes. They're like celestial stories that fill our night sky. Orion the Hunter, Ursa Major the Great Bear, and Cygnus the Swan are some of the characters in this starry tale.

But there's more to the Milky Way than just stars. It has its own traffic jams— highways of gas and dust stretching across space. These are called nebulae, and they're like clouds where new stars are born. Imagine these nebulae as cosmic construction sites, where stars are shaped over millions of years.

Nebula NGC 604

As we look at the night sky, we're seeing just a tiny part of the Milky Way. Our eyes can't capture the whole grandeur, but telescopes can. They've shown us that our galaxy is not alone—there are billions of other galaxies out there in the universe.

The Milky Way is a place of wonder and

discovery, where stars are born, live their lives, and sometimes even explode in bursts of light. It's like a cosmic theater where the drama of the universe unfolds. And even though it might seem distant and unreachable, it's our very own home, part of the amazing tapestry of the cosmos.

So, the next time you gaze up at the night sky and see the Milky Way, remember that you're looking at a tiny piece of a giant city of stars and mysteries.

Space Fact: The Milky Way has a supermassive black hole at its center, called Sagittarius A.* It has a mass of about 4 million times that of the sun and a diameter of about 22 million kilometers!

Sagittarius A*

Our Galactic Neighbors

Beyond our familiar Milky Way lie other galaxies. These galactic neighbors, though distant, offer glimpses into the vastness of the universe.

One such neighbor is the Andromeda Galaxy. It is the largest galaxy in the Local Group, a collection of about 54 galaxies that are gravitationally bound to each other. It is also the closest major galaxy to the Milky Way, at a distance of about 2.5 million light-years. It is much larger than our galaxy, with a diameter of about 220,000 light-years. It contains about one trillion stars, which is about twice as many stars as the Milky Way galaxy.

The Andromeda galaxy is moving toward the Milky

The Andromeda Galaxy

Way galaxy at a speed of about 250 kilometers per second. In about 4.5 billion years, the two galaxies are expected to collide and merge into a single, giant galaxy. The collision will be a violent event, but it is also likely to trigger a period of intense star formation.

Closer to home, there are the Large and Small Magellanic Clouds. These aren't clouds as we imagine them, but galaxies orbiting around the Milky Way. They are quite the sight in the southern hemisphere's night sky. These galaxies are much smaller than ours, and they're named after the explorer Ferdinand Magellan who spotted them during his travels.

Large and Small Magellanic Clouds

Space Fact: The Sagittarius Dwarf Irregular Galaxy is located about 70,000 light-years from Earth. It is currently in the process of being absorbed and torn apart by the gravitational forces of the Milky Way and has already lost a significant portion of its stars.

Stars and Black Holes

Every galaxy is made up of stars. They're like cosmic furnaces, producing heat and light through a process called nuclear fusion. This happens when hydrogen atoms join together, creating helium and releasing an immense amount of energy. Our sun is one such star, a ball of fire that warms our home planet.

Stars have their own life cycles. They are born from massive clouds of gas and dust. Gravity pulls these materials together, and when they become dense enough, nuclear fusion ignites, giving birth to a star.

As stars age, they change. Some grow bigger and become red giants, while others become smaller and cooler, turning into white dwarfs. In time, massive stars explode in an event called a supernova. These explosions can shine brighter than entire galaxies for a short while. What remains after a supernova is often a neutron star, where the star's mass is packed into a city-sized sphere.

Imagine a place where gravity is so strong that even light cannot escape—that's a black hole. When a massive star's core collapses under gravity's grip, it forms a black hole. These mysterious objects have such intense gravity that they warp space and time around them. Black holes might sound like science fiction, but they are real wonders in the cosmos.

Stars also have a color story to tell. The

color of a star depends on its temperature. Cooler stars appear red, warmer ones shine yellow like our sun, and the hottest stars blaze with a brilliant blue hue. These colors reveal what they are like inside and help astronomers learn more about the stars' lives.

One curious fact is that some of the stars we see in the sky might not actually exist anymore. Light takes time to travel, even from stars. So, when we look up at the night sky, we're often seeing stars as they were in the past. The light from the closest star to Earth, Proxima Centauri, takes more than four years to reach us.

Proxima Centauri

Space Fact: One teaspoon of a neutron star would weigh about 6 billion tons on Earth.

Exoplanets

Until very recently, no one knew for sure if the other stars in the universe had planets orbiting them. It was not until 1992 that the existence of an exoplanet was proven. In that year, two planets, Poltergeist and Phobetor were found orbiting a star called PSR B1257+12. Since then, we have found many more exoplanets by using different methods and tools. Some of these ways are watching the star's light get dimmer when the planet goes in front of it, watching the star move back and forth because of the planet's gravity, watching the star's light get brighter when the planet goes behind it or reflects its light, and watching the star's light get bent by the planet's gravity when they line up with us.

Now, there are over 5,000 confirmed exoplanets. One very common type is called a hot Jupiter. These are gas giant planets that are similar to Jupiter in size and mass, but much hotter and closer to their stars. They orbit their stars in just a few days or even hours, and have surface temperatures of thousands of degrees Celsius. They are also exposed to intense radiation and wind from their stars, which can strip away their atmospheres or make them glow.

Another common variety is called a super Earth. These are rocky planets that are larger than Earth but smaller than Neptune. They can have masses between two and ten times that of Earth. They can have different orbits and temperatures, depending on how far they are from their stars and how much heat they receive. Some super Earths may have thick atmospheres, oceans, or even life, while others may be dry, barren, or frozen. Super Earths are also very common in the galaxy, and they were first discovered in 2005. The first super

Earth ever found was Gliese 876 d, which is about 7 times as massive as Earth but only 1.2 times as big. It orbits its star every two days at a distance of only 3 million kilometers, which is 10 times closer than Mercury is to the sun.

In 2014, another super Earth called Kepler 186f was discovered. It is similar in size to Earth and is close enough to its sun that it is even possible that there is life on it.

Although the study of exoplanets is extremely difficult because of the huge interstellar distances involved are becoming an important new field in the study of astronomy.

Space Fact: An exoplanet called 55 Cancri e is made entirely out of diamond! On another planet, HD 189733 b, it rains glass sideways.

Part 2
Our Solar System

第2部 私たちの太陽系

　太陽系は、水素とヘリウムで構成されたガスと塵の渦巻く星雲の中から太陽が形成されたときに始まりました。太陽の周りに残っていたガスと塵の粒子が、徐々に集まって微惑星となり、微惑星は重力によってさらに粒子を引き寄せて大きくなることで最終的には惑星になりました。

【主な用語や表現】

ページ

33	planetesimal	微惑星
34	stickiness	粘着性
	asteroid	小惑星
35	G2-type star	スペクトル型G2型の主系列星
	yellow dwarf	黄色矮星
36	photosynthesize	光合成する
	envelop	包む, くるむ
	black dwarf	黒色矮星
38	axis	軸
	scorching-hot	焼け付くように暑い, やけどするほど熱い
	crater	隕石孔［クレーター］
	towering	そびえ立つ, 高くそびえる
39	solar wind	太陽風
40	shrouded	〜に覆われた, 〜に覆い隠された
	fiery	燃え盛る
41	inhospitable	荒涼たる, 生存に適さない
	hostile	敵意をもった
42	suffocating	息の詰まるような
43	Goldilocks zone	ゴルディロックス・ゾーン
	habitable	住むことができる, 住むのに適した
	magnetic field	磁場, 磁界
44	water vapor	水蒸気
	nitrogen	窒素

charged　電気を帯びた

deflect　屈折させる，ゆがめる，偏向させる

45　debris　デブリ，(破壊された物の)破片

46　basalt　玄武岩

47　moonquake　月震

48　harshness　厳しさ

robotic　ロボットの[のような・による]

rover　惑星探査機，ローバー

terrain　地形，地勢

Olympus Mons　オリンポス山

50　welcoming　快適な，心地良い

breathable　呼吸に適した

51　cloud-covered　雲におおわれた

Great Red Spot　(木星の)大赤斑

52　magnetism　磁気，磁性

collaborate　共同して働く，協力する

53　aurora　オーロラ

54　encircle　(〜を)(取り)囲む

gaseous　ガス(状)の

mesmerizing　魅惑する

55　showcase　見せる，展示する

contamination　汚染

56　methane　メタン

58　undiscovered　発見されていない

60　retrograde　(惑星や衛星が)逆行の

61　space probe　宇宙探査機

62　Kuiper Belt　カイパーベルト

63　dwarf planet　準惑星

64　criteria　基準

66　asteroid belt　小惑星帯

70　coma　コマ《彗星核の周囲を取り巻く星雲状のもの》

dust tail　ちりの尾

gas tail　(彗星の)ガスの尾

71　Comet NEOWISE　ネオワイズ彗星

Birth of the Solar System

About 4.5 billion years ago, there was nothing in this area of space but a swirling cloud of gas and dust, or nebula, mostly made up of hydrogen and helium. This nebula was slowly rotating. As it rotated, it began to collapse due to its own gravity. The collapse caused the nebula to heat up. The center of the nebula became so hot that nuclear fusion reactions began.

Nuclear fusion is a process that combines two or more atoms to form a heavier atom. The hydrogen atoms began fusing together to form helium atoms. This process releases a lot of energy.

From this collapse, our sun was born. It became a super-hot, glowing ball of fire that threw out incredible amounts of light and heat, warming up everything around it.

There were many tiny particles floating around the newly born sun. These were leftovers from the swirling cloud that hadn't been sucked into the sun.

Slowly, over a lot of time, these bits started sticking together, forming larger and larger pieces of matter called planetesimals. As these planetesimals got bigger, their gravity got stronger. This made them attract more particles, and they grew even more.

Eventually, some of these growing planetesimals got so big that their gravity became incredibly strong. This turned them into planets. There were quite a few of these planet-building sites, and each one had its own unique ingredients. Some planets got more rocky stuff, while others grabbed onto gases.

In the middle of all this planet-making, there were some leftovers—smaller bits and pieces that didn't turn into planets. These leftovers became the asteroids, comets, and other rocky bodies that you can sometimes see zooming around the sky.

That is how the solar system we know today was formed. It's like a cosmic puzzle where all the pieces fell into place over billions of years. The swirling cloud turned into a star, and the particles became planets, moons, and our other neighbors in space. It's a story of gravity, stickiness, and a huge amount of time.

Today, the solar system consists of the eight planets: Mercury, Venus, Earth, Mars, Jupiter, Saturn, Uranus, and Neptune, somewhere around 750 moons, and probably billions of asteroids and comets. Let's take a tour of the solar system.

> **Space Fact:** The solar system is huge. The distance between the Sun and the most distant planet, Neptune, is about 4.5 billion kilometers, but the solar system is much larger even than that!

The Sun

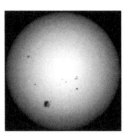

The Sun

Scientists classify the Sun as a G2-type star, or yellow dwarf, which means it is a medium-sized, middle-aged star. It is about 4.6 billion years old and has about 99.8 percent of the mass of the entire solar system. The Sun's diameter is about 1.4 million kilometers, which is about 109 times the diameter of Earth.

On the surface, the sun is about 5,500°C, but its core temperature is much hotter, at about 15 million °C. This is where nuclear fusion reactions take place, converting hydrogen into helium and releasing enormous amounts of energy.

The Sun's energy travels through space as light and heat. It takes about eight minutes for the Sun's light to reach Earth. This light is what powers life on Earth, providing plants with the energy they need to photosynthesize and animals with the energy they need to survive.

The Sun's gravity holds the planets, moons, and comets in their orbits, and its light and heat help to regulate the Earth's climate.

Scientists estimate that the sun will continue to shine for about another 5 billion years. After that, it will run out of hydrogen fuel and the core will begin to collapse. However, the rest of the sun will expand greatly, becoming a red giant. At this time, it will become so large that will envelop the inner planets, probably including Earth. It will remain a red giant for about a billion years and then become a white dwarf star, a much smaller and cooler star. Then, over the next trillion years or so, it will lose the rest of its heat and become a black dwarf, which is cold and gives off no energy.

Space Fact: The amount of energy released by the Sun in one second is more than humanity has used throughout history.

Mercury

Mercury

Mercury, named after the swift messenger of the ancient Roman gods moves around the sun at an incredible speed of 47 kilometers per second, and takes just 88 days to complete one orbit of our star. The reason Mercury orbits the Sun so fast is that it is the closest planet to the Sun. The Sun's gravity pulls on Mercury more than it does on any other planet, so Mercury has to move faster to stay in orbit.

While the years on Mercury are short, the days are extremely long. It spins slowly on its axis, meaning that a single day is the same amount of time as 59 days on Earth. Mercury has a diameter of about 4,880 kilometers, making it the smallest planet in the solar system.

It's a scorching-hot world during the day, where temperatures climb high enough to melt lead. But as night covers the planet, Mercury becomes freezing cold. This huge temperature swing is due to its thin blanket of air, which is unable to stop the heat from escaping.

One remarkable feature of Mercury is its rocky surface. It has been hit by countless meteorites, leaving behind scars called craters. As the Sun's rays touch these craters, they create long shadows, making Mercury's surface an incredible sight to see. Scientists believe that long ago, powerful volcanic eruptions formed its surface, creating vast plains and towering mountains all over its landscape.

Unlike Earth, Mercury's atmosphere is a thin layer of gases. The solar wind, a stream of charged paricles released from the Sun, has stripped Mercury of most of its atmosphere over millions of years, leaving it bare and exposed.

Because it is so close to the sun, Mercury has been difficult for scientists to study, but they hope to learn more about this mysterious planet in the future.

Space Fact: Mercury is smaller than Titan, one of the moons of Saturn.

Venus

Venus, the second planet from the Sun,

Venus

is visible after dusk or before dawn, earning it the names "Evening Star" and "Morning Star." It is named after Venus, the Roman goddess of love and beauty.

It has a diameter of about 12,000 kilometers, making it similar in size to Earth.

Venus is wrapped in a thick blanket of clouds, making it a mystery shrouded in mist. These clouds aren't soft and white like the ones found Earth's sky. Instead, they're made of acid and smell like rotten eggs. In addition, there are huge amounts of carbon dioxide in the atmosphere, and that traps heat, creating a greenhouse effect that is much more serious than the one we're currently experiencing on Earth. Daytime temperatures there can reach 475°C, making it hotter than Mercury, even though it's much farther from the sun.

The surface is a mix of vast plains and towering volcanic peaks. Imagine standing among fiery volcanoes and high mountains, surrounded by an atmosphere so dense that it feels like walking underwater.

Though Venus seems inhospitable, humans have attempted to discover its secrets. In the 20th century, spacecraft were sent to see what was beneath its thick clouds. These mechanical explorers discovered more about its hostile nature. Thirteen Soviet spacecraft, called *Venera*, braved the heat and pressure, sending back images of Venus's surface.

Venus's journey around the Sun takes about 225 Earth days, but its rotation is slow and strange. Unlike most planets, Venus spins in the opposite direction of its orbit. If you stood on its surface, the Sun would rise in the west and set in the east. A day on Venus, from sunrise to sunrise, takes longer than its year.

Neither Venus nor Mercury has a moon. This is believed to be because they are so close to the sun that its incredible gravity would capture anything circling around the planets.

As you consider Venus's mysteries, you might wonder if life could ever exist there. With its fiery surface and suffocating atmosphere, life as we know it would struggle to survive. Recently, though, researchers detected phosphine, a potential sign of life, in the upper clouds of Venus. While this discovery doesn't confirm life, it has created renewed interest in the planet and the possibility of life existing in some form.

Space Fact: Venus is the second brightest object in the night sky. Only the moon gives off more light.

Earth

Earth

Earth is unique from the other planets in our solar system in many ways. First of all, it is in what is known as the Goldilocks zone. The name comes from the fairy tale called Goldilocks and the Three Bears. The theme of the story is that things that are not too extreme are ideal, and the Goldilocks zone refers to a distance from a star where nothing is too hot or too cold so that water can exist in a liquid form and support life. Liquid water is essential for life as we know it, so the Goldilocks zone is the most likely place to find habitable planets.

We also have a thick atmosphere that protects us from the Sun's harmful radiation. In addition, Earth has a strong magnetic field that protects us from the solar wind.

Like the rest of the solar system's planets, Earth was formed about 4.5 billion years ago. Earth has a diameter of about 12,742 kilometers, making it the fifth-largest planet in the solar system. It was originally very hot, but it cooled over time. The water vapor in the atmosphere condensed and formed oceans. The rocks on the surface of Earth solidified, and the atmosphere became thinner.

Earth's atmosphere is made up of many different gases, including nitrogen, oxygen, and carbon dioxide. The atmosphere also helps to regulate the planet's temperature.

Earth has a strong magnetic field that protects us from the solar wind. The solar wind is a stream of charged particles from the Sun. The magnetic field deflects the solar wind away from Earth, and it helps to protect our atmosphere from being stripped away.

Life on Earth is thought to have arisen about 3.8 billion years ago. The first life forms were probably simple bacteria. Over time, life on Earth became more complex, giving rise to animals and plants, and eventually humans.

> **Space Fact:** Earth orbits the sun at an incredible speed of about 30 kilometers per second.

The Moon

Our moon is thought to have formed after a large object hit the Earth early in its history. The impact threw a lot of debris

The Moon

into space, and this debris eventually came together to form the Moon.

The moon is much smaller than Earth—its diameter is just 3,474 kilometers at its equator. The Moon is made up of mostly basalt, a type of rock that is also found on Earth. Its surface is covered in craters, which were formed by impacts from asteroids and comets. The Moon also has a few volcanoes, but they are much smaller than the ones on Earth.

The Moon lacks many of the things that are necessary for life. For one, it has almost no atmosphere, so it is very dry, and can be extremely cold. The temperature on the Moon is about -180°C at night. The Moon also has no liquid water on its surface, but there is ice. It also has an extremely weak magnetic field, so it is not protected from the Sun's harmful radiation.

The Moon's gravity is about one-sixth of that on Earth. This means astronauts can jump much higher on the Moon than they can here.

The Moon is very important to our planet.

It helps to stabilize the Earth's tilt, which helps to keep our temperatures moderate. The Moon also causes the tides, which are the regular rise and fall of the oceans.

Space Fact: The ground sometimes shakes on the moon, but they're called "moon-quakes" instead of "earthquakes."

Mars

Mars, the fourth planet from the sun, has long captured the human imagination. This rust-colored world, named after the Roman god of war due to its fiery

Mars

appearance, has been a subject of fascination for centuries.

Mars has a diameter of about 6,779 kilometers, making it the second-smallest planet in the solar system. Its reddish color comes from the iron-rich dust that covers its surface. While Earth's atmosphere shields us from the harshness of space, Mars has a thinner one, so it would be impossible for humans to breathe and survive there without special equipment.

Scientists have sent robotic explorers to Mars to learn more about its secrets. The rovers have journeyed across its rocky terrain, capturing pictures and collecting data. These mechanical travelers have shown us the planet's rugged landscape, with huge deserts, towering mountains, and the largest volcano in the solar system, Olympus Mons, which is 25 kilometers high. That's nearly

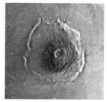

Olympus Mons

three times as high as Mt. Everest, which is 8.8 kilometers high.

One of the most interesting questions about Mars is whether it ever had the conditions to support life. Evidence suggests that Mars once had flowing water, possibly even lakes and rivers. Today, the only known water is in the form of ice at the planet's two poles. The presence of water is a key ingredient for life as we know it, so some scientists are hopeful that tiny organisms or signs of past life might be hidden beneath the surface. Discovering life on Mars would be an incredible breakthrough.

Mars's thin atmosphere has not stopped humanity from dreaming about sending astronauts there someday. This dream, however, is not without challenges. The journey to Mars is long, taking about seven months in the cold, dark vacuum of space.

Once on Mars, explorers would face a harsh environment. The thin atmosphere would require them to wear protective suits, shielding them from harmful radiation and extreme temperatures. The landscape would be their new frontier, where they could uncover the planet's history and seek out its hidden treasures.

While Mars holds many wonders, it's not a welcoming place for humans without advanced technology. The lack of breathable air, the thin atmosphere, and the extreme temperatures make survival challenging. However, human ingenuity knows no bounds, and the dream of setting foot on Mars remains.

 Space Fact: Mars's two moons, Phobos and Deimos, are thought to be captured asteroids.

(left) Phobos
(right) Deimos

Jupiter

Jupiter

Jupiter, named after the king of the Roman gods, is a giant ball of gas far larger than all the other planets combined. It has a diameter of about 139,822 kilometers.

A cloud-covered planet, Jupiter has beautiful bands of color when seen from space, and the colorful clouds create, constantly changing patterns. Its most well-known feature is its Great Red Spot, a swirling storm that has continued for centuries. This massive storm is like a timeless dance of color and chaos, caused

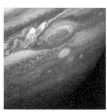

Jupiter's Great Red Spot

by the planet's extreme weather. Scientists study these storms to understand the complex forces at play within Jupiter's atmosphere.

51

Jupiter is a world of extremes, where size, gravity, and magnetism collaborate to create wonders. Its powerful gravity pulls objects into it, and this is very useful to Earth—it prevents many asteroids from coming too close to us. Jupiter is our protector, deflecting potential threats that could otherwise alter the course of our home planet.

Jupiter is surrounded by a large group of about 95 moons, each with its own character and mysteries. Some of these moons, like Europa and Ganymede, may have oceans below their surfaces, raising questions about the potential for life beyond Earth.

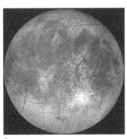
Europa

Ganymede

Jupiter's magnetic field is another marvel. It's like an invisible cloak, shielding the planet from the solar wind. This protective barrier creates powerful auroras, dancing curtains of light that paint the planet's polar skies.

Humanity's quest to explore Jupiter has been marked by bold missions. Spacecraft like *Voyager*, *Galileo*, and *Juno* have come close, transmitting images and data that have expanded our understanding of this giant world. These missions are like windows into the unknown, offering glimpses of the majesty and mysteries of the gas giant.

The Voyager spacecraft

Space Fact: The Great Red Spot on Jupiter was first observed in 1660s by Robert Hooke.

Saturn

Saturn

Saturn, named after the Roman god of agriculture, is best known for its incredible rings. These rings encircle the planet like cosmic decorations. They're not solid like hoops, but rather made of countless icy particles. Imagine looking up at the sky from Saturn. The rings would stretch far and wide, casting a soft glow on the landscape below.

Saturn is huge, making it one of the gas giants in our cosmic neighborhood. It has a diameter of about 116,460 kilometers.

Its atmosphere is a mixture of gases. This gaseous envelope gives Saturn its golden color, and its swirling patterns of clouds create a mesmerizing spectacle for distant observers.

Saturn has at least 145 moons, with the

possibility that more could be discovered in the future. Titan is the best known. It has a thick atmosphere, hiding secrets of complex

Titan

chemistry, much like during Earth's early days. Some scientists dream that exploring Titan might offer insights into the origins of life.

Cassini, a spacecraft sent from Earth, orbited Saturn for years, offering us a window into its wonders. The images it beamed back showcased the rings in incredible detail. *Cassini*'s journey ended with a bold move, diving into Saturn's atmosphere, causing it to melt in

order to protect potential life on its moons from contamination.

Cassini

Space Fact: The winds on Saturn blow at a speed of about 1,800 kilometers per hour.

Uranus

Uranus

Uranus, named after the ancient Greek sky god, is a distant neighbor in our solar system. It's the seventh planet from the sun, located beyond Saturn. Unlike its neighboring planets, Uranus spins on its side. Scientists speculate that a long-ago collision might have caused this unique spin.

Wrapped in layers of icy clouds, Uranus possesses a mysterious beauty. Its atmosphere is mostly made up of hydrogen and helium, but what sets it apart are the traces of methane. This methane is what gives Uranus its striking blue color. As sunlight enters the atmosphere, it reacts with the methane, scattering the blue light. It is also the coldest planet in the solar system, with temperatures as low as -244°C. Although it is not the most distant planet from the sun, because of its unusual tilt, its poles experience nights that are more than 40 years long, and this causes the extreme coldness.

Uranus has a diameter of about 50,724 kilometers, making it the third-largest planet in the solar system. Unlike its larger siblings, Jupiter and Saturn, Uranus isn't easily visible to the naked eye. People in the past, limited by their primitive telescopes, often mistook it for a star. It wasn't until the 18th century that Uranus was discovered to be a planet, thanks to the observations of astronomers using more-advanced instruments.

Like Saturn, Uranus boasts a beautiful system of rings. While faint compared with Saturn's, they are amazing in their own right. Made of bits of ice and dust, they encircle the planet, whispering tales of the planet's distant past and the cosmic forces that shaped its rings.

Uranus is accompanied by a collection of 27 moons, each with its own story. Among them, Miranda stands out, with a surface that seems to bear many scars. Its rough terrain suggests that it experienced dramatic events in its history, per-

Miranda

haps a collision with a gigantic asteroid, or it may have been formed from the debris of other moons that collided with one another.

As humans ventured into the final frontier, Uranus became a destination of curiosity. Space-craft like *Voyager 2* have flown through space, observing this distant planet and its moons. These missions have revealed some of the planet's secrets, yet much remains undiscovered.

Space Fact: There are sometimes diamond rains on Uranus. When the methane molecules break down, the resulting carbon atoms form diamond crystals that rain down from the sky.

Neptune

Neputine

Neptune is the eighth and final planet in our solar system, a distant neighbor to Earth and the other seven planets that revolve around the Sun. It takes a spacecraft several years to reach Neptune, as it orbits the Sun in a long orbit that lasts nearly 165 Earth years.

Neptune's most distinctive feature is its incredible blue color. The gaseous atmosphere of Neptune contains elements that absorb red light and reflect blue light, giving the planet its vibrant hue.

Neptune has a diameter of about 49,244 kilometers, making it the fourth-largest planet in the solar system.

A gas giant, Neptune is composed mostly of hydrogen and helium. Its atmosphere is an incredible dance of fast-moving clouds and powerful storms. The Great Dark Spot, a massive storm system similar to Jupiter's Great Red Spot, was once observed on Neptune's surface.

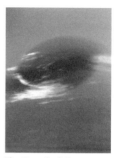

The Great Dark Spot

Neptune's weather is more than just violent winds and swirling clouds. The planet experiences some of the strongest winds in the solar system, reaching speeds of up to 2,000 kilometers per hour, which is faster than the speed of sound! These powerful winds, combined with the extremely cold temperatures, create an environment that would be nearly impossible for humans to survive in.

Neptune also has a collection of 14 moons. Triton, the largest, is particularly fascinating. Unlike most moons in the solar system, Triton orbits Neptune in a backward, or retrograde, motion. This unusual behavior suggests that Triton might not have originated near Neptune, but rather was captured by the planet's

Triton

gravitational pull in the distant past.

As we explore Neptune, we must also mention its ring system. While not as easy to see as Saturn's, Neptune's rings are composed of dusty particles and icy fragments. These rings add a touch of elegance to the planet's appearance, sparkling in the distant sunlight.

Journeying to Neptune requires a tremendous amount of technology and innovation, and so far, *Voyager 2* is the only space probe that has visited this distant planet.

Space Fact: Although Galileo was the first person to see Neptune, he thought it was a star, so he is not credited with its discovery.

The Kuiper Belt

The Kuiper Belt is a region of icy objects that lies beyond the orbit of Neptune. It is a very cold place, with temperatures that can reach as low as -230°C. It is also very dark, with only a few faint stars visible.

The Kuiper Belt is thought to be a remnant of the early solar system. When the solar system was young, it was a very hot place. The heat caused the material to spread out, and it formed a disk around the sun. This disk was made up of dust, gas, and ice.

Over time, the disk cooled down. The dust and gas clumped together to form planets. The ice, however, did not clump together as easily. It was too cold, and it was too spread out.

Some of the ice, however, did clump together to form small bodies. These bodies were too small to be planets, but they were big enough to be called dwarf planets. The Kuiper Belt is made up of these dwarf planets, including Pluto, and other small icy bodies, including asteroids.

Scientists are still learning about the Kuiper Belt. They believe that it may be home to many new worlds, including objects that are larger than Pluto.

Space Fact: There are believed to be over 100,000 objects in the Kuiper Belt.

Pluto

Pluto, named for the Roman god of the dead, is a small, icy world that was once considered the ninth

Pluto

planet in our solar system. However, in 2006, the International Astronomical Union (IAU) decided that Pluto was actually a dwarf planet. This was because Pluto does not meet all of the IAU's criteria for a planet. A planet must be in orbit around the sun, be massive enough that its own gravity has pulled it into a round shape, and have cleared the neighborhood around its orbit. Pluto does not meet the third condition because it shares its orbit with many other objects, such as the Kuiper Belt objects.

Even though Pluto is not a planet, it is still a very interesting and mysterious world. With a diameter of 2,376 km, it is the largest known dwarf planet in our solar system, and it has a unique atmosphere that is made up of nitrogen, methane, and carbon monoxide. Pluto also has a heart-shaped region on its surface, which is made up of frozen nitrogen.

In 2015, the *New Horizons* spacecraft flew past Pluto and gave us our first close-up look at the dwarf planet. *New Horizons* revealed that Pluto is a much more complex and diverse world than we had previously thought. It has mountains, valleys, plains, and craters. It also has five moons, including Charon, which is about half the size of Pluto.

New Horizons

Charon

Pluto is a fascinating world, and we are still learning about it. It is a reminder that there is still much that we do not know about our solar system.

Space Fact: Pluto is usually farther away from the Sun than Neptune, but because of the unusual shape of its orbit, sometimes it comes closer.

Dwarf Planets

Ceres

In addition to Pluto, there are four other dwarf planets in our solar system: Ceres, Eris, Makemake, and Haumea. All of them are in the Kuiper Belt except for Ceres, which is in the asteroid belt

Makemake

between Mars and Jupiter. Ceres is about the size of France, and it is made up of mostly rock and ice. It is thought that it could have become a planet, but the powerful gravity of Jupiter prevented it from larger.

Eris is the second-largest dwarf planet in the Kuiper Belt. It is slightly smaller in diameter than Pluto, but it has a larger mass. Eris was discovered in 2005, and it caused a lot of controversy because it was initially thought to be the tenth planet in our solar system. The difficulty in deciding whether it was a planet or not was what led to Pluto being classified as a dwarf planet.

Space Fact: There may be other dwarf planets that have not been discovered yet. Some experts think that there may be as many as 200 in the Kuiper Belt.

Asteroids

Asteroids are small, rocky bodies that orbit the sun. They are thought to be the remnants of the early solar system, when the planets were forming. They are mainly found in the asteroid belt, which lies between the orbits of Mars and Jupiter. This belt is also the boundary between the inner rocky planets like Earth and Mars, and the gas giants, like Saturn and Jupiter.

Asteroids in this region range in size from a few meters to hundreds of kilometers in diameter. It is thought that there could be up to 1.9 million asteroids larger than 1 kilometer in diameter there, as well as countless smaller ones.

Asteroids can also be dangerous. It is thought that in 1908, an asteroid exploded over Tunguska, Siberia, and caused a massive explosion that flattened forests over an area of about 2,000 square kilometers.

Space Fact: Some asteroids have their own moons. There is an asteroid located between Mars and Jupiter that has its own moon named Dactyl.

Comets

Comets are some of the most amazing and mysterious objects in space. These giant balls of ice and dust travel around the Sun in long, oval-shaped paths. Sometimes, they come very close to the Sun and Earth, and we can see them in the sky with our eyes or telescopes.

Comets are leftovers from the time when the Sun and the planets were formed, about 4.6 billion years ago. They are mostly made of frozen water, carbon dioxide, ammonia, and methane, mixed with rocks and dust. They are very cold and hard when they are far away from the Sun, but when they get closer, they start to heat up and melt. This is when they become visible to us.

As a comet approaches the Sun, some of its ice turns into gas and escapes from its surface. This gas forms a huge cloud around the comet's core. The cloud is called the coma, and it can be bigger than a planet! The Sun's light makes the coma glow brightly, and the Sun's wind pushes some of the gas and dust away from the comet. This creates a long tail that stretches behind the comet for millions of kilometers.

Comets actually have two tails: one made of dust and one made of gas. The dust tail is white and curved, and it follows the comet's path. The gas tail is blue and straight, and it points away from the Sun. Sometimes, we can see both tails with our eyes, but other times we need special instruments to see them.

There are many comets in space, but only a few of them are famous. One of them is

Halley's Comet

Comet NEOWISE

Halley's Comet, which visits the Sun every 76 years. The last time it was here was in 1986, and the next time will be in 2061. Another one is Comet NEOWISE, which was discovered in 2020 by a NASA telescope. It was very bright and beautiful in July 2020, but it will not return for another 6,800 years!

Space Fact: The chances of Earth being hit by a comet in a year are very low—about 1 in 300,000.

Part 3
Space Exploration

第3部　宇宙探査

　宇宙探査は、人類の夢と挑戦です。新しい技術や資源を使って、私たちは宇宙の謎や美しさを探求しています。宇宙探査は、私たちに新しい知識や発見をもたらすだけでなく、地球の問題に対する解決策や視点も提供します。そして、私たちは自分自身と宇宙の一部であることを再認識できます。

【主な用語や表現】

nanometer　ナノメートル

103　laws of physics　物理法則

104　medium Earth orbit (MEO)　中軌道

navigation satellite　航行衛星

geostationary orbit (GEO)　静止軌道

communication(s) satellite　通信衛星

cosmic ray　宇宙線

105　natural phenomena　自然現象

eclipse　月食，日食

light pollution　光害

space junk　宇宙ゴミ

artificial object　人工物体

rocket stage　ロケットのステージ［段階］

106　functioning　機能する

chain reaction　連鎖反応

Kessler syndrome　ケスラーシンドローム

107　hydrazine　ヒドラジン《ロケット・ジェットエンジンの燃料》

implement　実行する，道具［手段］を提供する

tracking　（痕跡などを）たどること，追う［追跡する］こと

stakeholder　利害関係者

sustainability　持続可能性

108　unmanned　無人（操縦）の

109　fly by　〜に接近飛行する

110　composition　組織，組成，構成

111　solar flare　太陽フレア

re-entry　（宇宙船などの大気圏への）再突入

Mars rover　マーズ・ローバー，火星探査車

112　wheeled　車輪の付いた，車輪で動く

113　spectrometer　分光器

114　dust storm　砂塵あらし

115　habitability　居住適性

117 space age　宇宙時代

　　detonate　爆発させる

118 artificial radiation belt　人工放射線帯

　　inconclusive　決定的でない

　　megaton　メガトン

　　fireball　火球

119 Outer Space Treaty　宇宙条約

　　mass destruction　大量破壊

　　anti-satellite weapons (ASATs)　衛星攻撃兵器

　　ballistic missile defense systems (BMDs)　弾道ミサイル
　　防衛システム

　　directed energy weapons (DEWs)　指向性エネルギー兵
　　器

　　kinetic energy　運動エネルギー

　　Space Force　宇宙軍

122 brain-computer interface　ブレイン・コンピューター・イ
　　ンターフェース

　　multi-planetary　多惑星の

123 payload　ペイロード《(宇宙船に搭載される)観測機器, 実験
　　装置》

　　deep space　深宇宙

　　heavy-lift　ヘビーリフト［重量物運搬］

124 underserved　十分なサービスを受けていない

　　orbital rocket booster　軌道ロケットブースター

127 surveillance　監視, 監督, 見張り

　　orbital debris　軌道上デブリ

　　cyberattack　サイバー攻撃

130 stopover point　中継地

131 near-Earth asteroid　地球近傍小惑星

　　robotic spacecraft　無人宇宙船, 宇宙ロボット

　　interstellar travel　恒星間旅行

Ancient Dreams and Early Discoveries

The quest to understand the cosmos began long ago. In ancient times, people looked up at the night sky, observing the twinkling stars and the mysterious movements of planets. Many ancient peoples believed that they were looking up at heaven or that things like comets or meteors were a sign that something terrible was going to happen on Earth.

As years passed, these dreams of understanding led to significant discoveries. Ancient civilizations like the Babylonians and Greeks noticed patterns in the sky and mapped the movements of the stars and planets. They marked the passage of time through the changing positions of these celestial bodies, helping them predict seasons and navigate the seas.

Space Fact: Stars twinkle because their light passes through Earth's atmosphere. Differences in temperature and density cause it to bend slightly, and this causes its brightness to change. In space, where there is no atmosphere, stars do not twinkle.

The Birth of Telescopes

In the early seventeenth century, a new tool changed the way we looked at the cosmos: the telescope. With its invention, astronomers like Galileo Galilei could look up into the heavens and see things that no one had ever imagined. Galileo's observations changed many old beliefs. He saw that

Galileo Galilei

Jupiter had its own moons, challenging the idea that all objects in space circled around Earth. This discovery raised fresh questions about the nature of the universe.

As time passed, more-powerful telescopes allowed us to view distant galaxies, causing scientists to realize that our Milky Way was just one among countless stars. Scientists like Edwin Hubble observed galaxies moving away from each other, revealing an astonishing truth: the universe is expanding.

Edwin Hubble

Space Fact: The telescope is believed to have been invented by a man named Hans Lipperhey in 1608.

Early Rocket Pioneers

The earliest rockets were used as weapons in China as early as the thirteenth century. These were made of bamboo tubes filled with gunpowder. Later, in the nineteenth

Konstantin Tsiolkovsky

century, a Russian physicist named Konstantin Tsiolkovsky developed what is called "the rocket equation," which was necessary for the modern rockets that we use today. He showed that the speed of a rocket can be calculated using things like the mass of the fuel burned and the force that the exhaust gases will produce. This principle is still used today in the design of rockets. Tsiolkovsky also developed the concept of the multistage rocket, which is a rocket that uses multiple stages to reach high altitudes. He is also known for saying, "Earth is the cradle of humanity, but one cannot remain in the cradle forever."

Another major breakthrough in space exploration came in 1926, when Robert Goddard used Tsiolkovsky's ideas to launch the first liquid-fueled rocket. This was an incredible achievement, as it showed that we could now build rockets that were powerful enough to reach space.

Robert Goddard and His Rocket

Space Fact: To escape from Earth's gravity, a rocket must travel at about 40,000 kilometers per hour.

War and Rockets

Wernher von Braun

Sadly, the next breakthrough in space exploration came at a terrible price. During World War II, Hitler and the Nazis recruited a brilliant scientist named Wernher von Braun to build rockets that would be used as weapons. Wernher's rocket was called the V-2 and was the first human-made object to travel into space. The V-2 was used to hit distant targets, and the attacks resulted in the deaths of about 2,700 people. However, the V-2 also had a significant impact on the development of space exploration, paving the way for the development of artificial satellites and manned spaceflight.

V-2 Rocket

After World War II, von Braun was brought to the United States. There is strong evidence that he was a war criminal, but he was also a brilliant scientist. Von Braun worked for NASA for many years, and was responsible for the development of the American space program, including the *Saturn V* rocket, which was used to launch the Apollo missions to the moon. Von Braun was a visionary leader, and he played a major role in the development of space exploration.

Saturn V

In the years following World War II, the Western world, led by the United States, confronted the communist nations of the USSR, and rockets and missiles were a huge part of the competition. The main difference between a rocket and a missile is what it is carrying. If it has astronauts or a satellite aboard, then it is a rocket, and if it has explosives or a nuclear bomb on it, then it is a missile. Both sides wanted to explore space, but it was deeply connected with the struggle between communism and democracy.

Space Fact: The *Saturn V* rocket burned more fuel in one second than Charles Lindbergh used when he made the first solo crossing of the Atlantic Ocean.

Sputnik 1 and Yuri Gagarin

Sputnik 1

In 1957 the USSR launched *Sputnik 1*, the first artificial satellite to orbit Earth. The United States was not prepared for the launch of *Sputnik*, and it was seen as a major victory for the Soviet Union. This evidence that the USSR was so far ahead in space technology led to a new sense of urgency in the United States. Then,

Yuri Gagarin

in 1961, the Soviet Union achieved another major milestone in the Space Race. Yuri Gagarin became the first human to orbit Earth. Gagarin's flight was another major victory for the Soviet Union. It made the US realize that it needed to do something dramatic to narrow the USSR's lead in space. The government increased funding for the space program, and it started to develop new rockets and spacecraft.

Space Fact: *Sputnik* had a diameter of just 58 centimeters, about the size of a beach ball.

The Apollo Program and the First Moon Landing

John F. Kennedy

In 1962, President John F. Kennedy announced that the United States was going to put a man on the moon before the end of the decade. Thus began the Apollo program, one of the most daring and ambitious projects in human history.

The Apollo program involved thousands of engineers, scientists, technicians, and astronauts who worked together to design, build, test, and operate the spacecraft and equipment needed for the lunar missions. The program faced many challenges and setbacks, such as budget limitations, technical difficulties, and

Apollo 1 Command Module

terrible accidents. One of the most horrible moments was the *Apollo 1* fire, which killed three astronauts during a pre-launch test in 1967. The program also had to overcome public criticism, as some people questioned the value and morality of spending so much money on space exploration.

Despite these obstacles, the Apollo program continued. The first manned flight in the Apollo program was *Apollo 7* in 1968, which tested the command and service module in Earth orbit. The next milestone came that same year, when *Apollo 8* became the first manned spacecraft to leave Earth orbit and circle the moon.

Apollo 8: Earthrise

The astronauts who participated in the Apollo missions faced many risks and challenges, such as launch failures, radiation exposure, equipment malfunctions, and dangers on the moon. They also had to endure long periods of isolation, stress, and physical discomfort.

Apollo 11 Crew

Finally, the moment of truth arrived. *Apollo 11* was launched on July 16, 1969, with three astronauts on board: Neil Armstrong, Edwin "Buzz" Aldrin, and Michael Collins. After four days of traveling through space, Armstrong and Aldrin separated from Collins and entered the lunar module, named *Eagle*, for their descent to the moon. The descent was

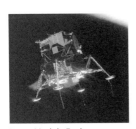
Lunar Module Eagle

extremely dangerous, and the *Eagle* had only a few seconds worth of fuel left when it landed on a flat area in the Sea of Tranquility.

Armstrong radioed back to Earth: "Houston, Tranquility Base here. The Eagle has landed."

About six hours later, Armstrong opened the hatch and stepped out of the lunar module. He became the first human to walk on the moon. He spoke his famous words: "That's one small step for [a] man, one giant leap for mankind." Aldrin

Neil Armstrong - First Moon Landing

soon joined him outside, and they spent about two hours on the lunar surface. They collected rocks, planted a flag, talked to President Richard Nixon on Earth, and left behind a plaque that read: "Here men from the planet Earth first set foot upon the moon July 1969 A.D. We came in peace for all mankind."

After rejoining Collins in orbit, they began their journey back to Earth. They came down in the Pacific Ocean on July 24, 1969. They were greeted by cheering crowds and honored by parades and ceremonies around the world.

The Apollo program continued with six more missions to the moon until 1972. Twelve men walked on the moon in total, exploring different regions and conducting various experiments. They

Apollo 17

also brought back about 382 kilograms of lunar rocks and soil samples for scientific analysis. The last mission was *Apollo 17*. It was the end of an era.

The Apollo program was a testament to human curiosity, creativity, and ambition. It was also a victory for the United States in the Space Race, as it achieved what the Soviet Union could not: landing humans on the moon and bringing them back safely. The Soviet program, which had been plagued by internal rivalries, political interference, and lack of funding, was unable to launch its own manned lunar mission before the United States. The Soviet program then shifted its focus to developing space stations and robotic missions to other planets. The Soviet space program continued until the end of the Soviet Union in 1991, after which it was reorganized as the Russian space program.

Space Fact: The footprints left by Apollo astronauts on the Moon will probably remain for millions of years due to the lack of erosion.

The Space Shuttle

The space shuttle was a reusable spacecraft that

Space Shuttle

was first launched by the United States in 1981. It was designed to carry up to eight people and a large amount of cargo into low Earth orbit.

The space shuttle was a major technological achievement because it took off like a rocket, but it could be landed like an airplane. Because it could be reused, it was thought that this would save a lot of money. In reality, though, it turned out to be far more expensive than ordinary rockets. It did, however, make it possible to launch the Hubble Space Telescope and construct the International Space Station.

Sadly, there were two tragic accidents involving space shuttles, the *Challenger* Disaster in 1986 and the *Columbia* Disaster in 2003, in which the entire crews of both spacecraft were killed.

Challenger Disaster

However, NASA and the astronauts carried on despite the

tragedies, and the space shuttle remained a versatile spacecraft that played a major role in space exploration until 2011.

> **Space Fact:** It is estimated that the Space Shuttle program cost about $209 billion. Since there were 134 flights, that's about $1.6 billion per flight.

The International Space Station

The International Space Station, or ISS for short, is a huge structure that orbits

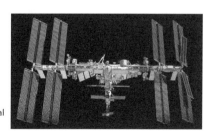

The International
Space Station

around the Earth. It is like a home and a laboratory in space, where astronauts from different countries live and work together. The ISS is one of the most amazing and important achievements of humanity in space exploration.

The ISS is the largest and heaviest object that humans have ever put into space. It is longer than a soccer field and weighs more than 300 cars. It has many parts, including modules, trusses, solar arrays, and robotic arms. The modules are where the astronauts live and do experiments. The trusses are the metal beams that hold the solar arrays, which are the panels that collect sunlight and turn it into electricity. The robotic arms are used to move things around and help with repairs.

Because it is so big, the ISS could not be launched as one piece. Instead, many pieces were joined together in space. It took more than 40 flights by rockets and space shuttles to bring all the parts to orbit. The first piece was launched in 1998, and the last piece was added in 2021. The ISS is always changing, as new parts and experiments are added or removed.

The ISS orbits around the Earth at a speed of about 28,000 kilometers per hour. That means it goes around the Earth once every 90 minutes. Sometimes, the ISS passes over your location, and you can see it in the night sky as a bright star moving fast. No matter where you are in the world, you can use a website like https://spotthestation.nasa.gov/ to find out when and where to look for it.

Ever since November 2000, the ISS has been continuously occupied. More than 240 people from 19 countries have visited it so far. The crew usually consists of six or seven astronauts from different countries, such as the United States, Russia, Japan, Canada, Italy, France, and Germany. They stay on board for about six months at a time, and then return to Earth on a spacecraft. Sometimes, more people are on board during crew changes or special visits.

The main purpose of the ISS is to do scientific research in space. The astronauts conduct experiments in many fields, such as biology, physics, medicine, and astronomy. They study how living things and materials behave in microgravity. They also test new technologies and equipment that could be useful for future space missions. Some of the experiments are inside the modules, while others are outside on the trusses or platforms.

The ISS is also a place where humans learn how to live and work in space for long periods of time. The astronauts have to deal with many challenges and risks, such as isolation, radiation, extreme temperatures, space debris, and more. It is also important for them to exercise every day to keep their muscles and bones healthy. They have to eat special food that is dried or canned, but unfortunately, food does not taste as good in space.

The ISS is a remarkable example of international cooperation and peaceful exploration of space. It shows what humans can achieve when they work together for a common goal. It also inspires us to learn more about our planet and our universe. The ISS is not only a space station, but also a symbol of hope.

Space Fact: The astronauts on the ISS see 16 sunrises and sunsets every day!

Modern Telescopes

Telescopes are amazing devices that allow us to see far beyond what our eyes can. They help us explore the wonders of the universe, from planets and stars to galaxies and black holes.

They work by collecting and focusing light from distant objects. Light is a form of electromagnetic radiation that travels in waves, and different types of light have different wavelengths and frequencies, such as visible light, infrared light, ultraviolet light, X-rays, and radio waves. While some types of light can be seen by our eyes, others cannot. Telescopes use lenses or mirrors to gather more light than our eyes can, and then magnify the image for us to see.

There are two main types of telescopes: optical and non-optical. Optical telescopes use lenses or mirrors to focus visible light. They can be divided into refracting telescopes, which use lenses, and reflecting telescopes, which use mirrors. Refracting telescopes were the first type of telescope invented, and they are still used today for small observations. Reflecting telescopes are more common and more powerful, as they can use large mirrors and avoid some problems caused by lenses.

Non-optical telescopes use other types of detectors to focus non-visible light, such as radio waves, infrared waves, X-rays, or gamma rays. These types of light can reveal different aspects of the universe that optical telescopes cannot see. For example, radio telescopes can detect signals from distant galaxies and quasars, infrared telescopes can see through dust and gas clouds, X-ray telescopes can observe hot objects like neutron stars and black holes, and gamma-ray telescopes can study the most energetic events in the universe.

Some telescopes are located on the ground, while others are launched into space. Ground-based telescopes have some advantages, such as being cheaper, easier to maintain, and able to use larger mirrors or antennas. However, they also have some disadvantages, such as being affected by the Earth's atmosphere, weather, pollution, and light pollution. Space-based telescopes avoid the Earth's atmosphere, observe the whole sky, and detect more types of light. However, they are more expensive, are harder to repair, and are limited by size and weight.

One of the most famous space-based telescopes is the Hubble Space Telescope (HST), which was launched in 1990 by NASA and the European Space Agency. The HST is an optical telescope that uses a 2.4-meter mirror to observe visible, ultraviolet, and near-infrared light. The HST has made many amazing discoveries and images, such as the Hubble Deep Field (HDF), which shows thousands of galaxies in a

The Hubble Space Telescope

The Hubble Deep Field

tiny patch of sky, and the Pillars of Creation (POC), which are giant columns of gas and dust where stars are born.

The Pillars of Creation

Another space-based telescope called the James Webb Space Telescope (JWST), was launched in 2021. The JWST is an infrared telescope that uses a 6.5-meter mirror. The JWST has already made

The JWST spacecraft

some amazing discoveries, such as the most distant star ever seen, and it is expected to make many more in the years to come.

Space Fact: The mirror for the Hubble Space Telescope had to be polished for more than a year to give it an accuracy of 10 nanometers. That's about 1/10,000 the width of a human hair.

Satellites

Circling high above us are thousands of satellites that most people never think about, but which are essential for our daily lives. They provide us with data for weather forecasts, warn us of approaching typhoons, carry our cell phone signals, allow us to navigate using GPS, give us internet access in remote locations, broadcast TV signals, and more. They are also used by scientists to do research on things like global warming, and by the military to keep watch on other nations.

Artificial satellites orbit at different heights and speeds, depending on their mission and the laws of physics. The lowest orbit is called low Earth orbit (LEO), which ranges from 200 to 2,000 kilometers above Earth's surface. This is where most artificial satellites operate, such as the International Space Station (ISS), which orbits at about 400 kilometers above Earth.

The next orbit is called medium Earth orbit (MEO). It ranges from 2,000 to 35,786 kilometers above Earth's surface. This is where some navigation satellites operate, such as the Global Positioning System (GPS), which orbits about 20,000 kilometers above Earth.

The highest orbit is called geostationary orbit (GEO), which is exactly 35,786 kilometers above Earth's equator. This is where some communication satellites operate, such as television and radio satellites. These satellites appear to be stationary from Earth's perspective because they orbit at the same speed as Earth's rotation.

While artificial satellites have many benefits for humanity and society, they also have some drawbacks and challenges. They cost a lot of money and resources to build and launch, can malfunction or get damaged by space debris or cosmic rays, sometimes

interfere with each other or with natural phenomena such as auroras or eclipses, and can
also create environmental problems such as
light pollution or space junk.

Space Fact: In 2012, a satellite discovered that there are twice as many emperor
penguins in Antarctica as had previously been
believed.

Space Junk

Space junk is a term that refers to the artificial
objects that orbit the Earth and no longer serve
any useful purpose. These objects can range
from tiny pieces of paint to large satellites
and rocket stages. Space junk poses a serious
threat to both the environment and the future
of space exploration.

One of the main effects of space junk is the risk of collision with active satellites and spacecraft. According to the European Space Agency, there are millions of pieces of debris in orbit. These objects can travel at speeds of up to 28,000 kilometers per hour, making them capable of causing severe damage or even destroying spacecraft. For example, in 2009, an old Russian satellite collided with a functioning American satellite, creating thousands of new fragments. Such collisions can also trigger a chain reaction known as the Kessler syndrome, where the debris density becomes so high that collisions become inevitable and uncontrollable.

Another effect of space junk is the potential impact on Earth's environment. A proportion of the space junk in low Earth orbit will gradually lose altitude and burn up in Earth's atmosphere; larger debris, however, can occasionally impact Earth and have harmful effects on the environment. For instance, in 1978, a Soviet nuclear-powered satellite called *Kosmos 954* crashed in Canada, spreading radioactive debris over a large area. Moreover, some space junk may contain hazardous materials, such as hydrazine, which can contaminate soil and water if they reach the ground.

Space junk is a growing problem that requires urgent attention and action. Several plans have been proposed or implemented to deal with the issue, such as improving tracking and monitoring systems, designing more-sustainable spacecraft, implementing international regulations and guidelines, and developing active removal methods. However, these solutions face many technical, economic, legal, and political challenges. Therefore, it is essential to raise awareness and encourage cooperation among all stakeholders to ensure the safety and sustainability of the space environment.

Space Fact: NASA is currently monitoring about 50,000 pieces of space junk to make sure that it does not interfere with rockets or satellites.

Space Probes

While sending humans into space is dramatic and may one day make it possible for us to live on other planets, it is also extremely dangerous and expensive. A far cheaper, safer, and more efficient way to explore space is by using unmanned probes. These are special types of spacecraft that are sent to explore specific places or objects in space. They are different from satellites, which orbit around the Earth or other planets, and from rovers, which land and move on the surface of planets or moons.

Space probes fly by, orbit, or land on their targets, and then send back data and images to Earth.

Mariner 10

There are many types of space probes that have different missions and destinations. For example, *Mariner 10* was the first probe to fly by

Magellan

Mercury, *Magellan* was the first probe to map Venus, *Viking 1* and *2* were the first probes to land on Mars, *Galileo* was the first probe to orbit Jupiter, *Cassini* was the first probe to orbit Saturn, *Voyager 2* was the first probe to fly by Uranus and Neptune, and *New Horizons* was the first probe to fly by Pluto.

Viking

Hayabusa

25143 Itokawa

Another remarkable asteroid probe is *Hayabusa*. *Hayabusa* was launched in 2003 by JAXA, the Japanese space agency. Its mission was to visit an asteroid named Itokawa. *Hayabusa* arrived at Itokawa in 2005 and spent three months studying it from orbit. It took pictures and measured its shape, gravity, spin, temperature, and composition.

Hayabusa managed to land on Itokawa and collected some dust particles. It left in 2007 and returned to Earth in 2010 with a small capsule containing about 1,500 grains of asteroid material. This was the first time that a space probe returned samples from an asteroid.

Hayabusa's mission was not easy or smooth. It faced many challenges and problems along the way, such as fuel leaks, communication failures, solar flares, battery issues, and re-entry difficulties. However, *Hayabusa* overcame all these obstacles and inspired many young Japanese people to be interested in space exploration.

Space Fact: Hayabusa means "falcon" in English.

Mars Rovers

Mars rovers are special types of robots that are sent to land and travel around on the surface of Mars. They are like our eyes and ears on the Red Planet, which is a fascinating but hostile world. The rovers are wheeled vehicles with cameras, antennas, sensors, and instruments that allow them to navigate, communicate, and conduct scientific experiments. They are launched by rockets from Earth and travel millions of miles to reach Mars. They have to land safely on the surface, which is very tricky and dangerous. Then, they have to avoid obstacles, such as rocks, craters, and cliffs. Another serious problem is dust, which can cover their solar panels and reduce their power. They also have to cope with malfunctions, which can affect their performance or even end their mission.

There have been several Mars rovers that have explored different parts of Mars. The first one was *Sojourner*, which was part of the *Pathfinder* mission in 1997. It was a small

Sojourner

rover that weighed only 10.6 kilograms and was about the size of a microwave oven. It explored an area of about 100 meters around its landing site and took pictures, measured the weather, and analyzed the rocks and soil.

The next rovers were *Spirit* and *Opportunity*, which were part of the Mars Exploration Rover (MER) mission in 2004. They were twin rovers that weighed about 180

Opportunity

kilograms each and were about the size of a golf cart. The two rovers landed on opposite sides of Mars and explored different regions. They had cameras, spectrometers, magnets, microscopes, drills, and more. They searched for signs of water and past life on Mars, and also studied the geology and climate of the planet.

Spirit operated for more than six years and traveled more than 7 kilometers. It climbed hills, crossed craters, and got stuck in sand traps. It also found evidence of ancient hot springs and volcanic activity on Mars.

Opportunity operated for more than 14 years and traveled more than 45 kilometers. It broke many records for distance, endurance, and discovery on Mars. It also found evidence of ancient lakes and rivers.

Opportunity was very popular among people on Earth. It had many fans who followed its adventures online and on social media. *Opportunity*'s last message to Earth was "My battery is low and it's getting dark". It said this after a huge dust storm blocked its solar panels in 2018. Many people were sad when they heard this message, but they also celebrated *Opportunity*'s achievements and legacy.

In 2012, a new rover called *Curiosity*, which is part of the Mars Science Laboratory

(MSL) mission, landed. It is a large rover that weighs about 900 kilograms and is about the size of a car. It landed in a crater called Gale and has been explor-

Curiosity

ing its surroundings ever since. It has cameras, lasers, spectrometers, detectors, drills, scoops, ovens, and more. It aims to study the habitability and history of Mars. *Curiosity* also looks for organic molecules and evidence of ancient life on Mars.

The newest rovers on Mars are *Perseverance* and *Zhurong*. *Perseverance* is part of the Mars 2020 mission by NASA. It is similar to *Curiosity* but has some new features, such as

Perseverance

Zhurong

115

a helicopter drone called *Ingenuity*, a microphone to record sounds on Mars, and a system to collect and store rock samples for future return to Earth. *Perseverance* is also looking for signs of ancient life on Mars.

Ingenuity

Tianwen-1

Zhurong is part of the *Tianwen-1* mission by CNSA, the Chinese space agency. It is China's first Mars rover and landed in a plain called Utopia Planitia. It studies the surface features, soil characteristics, magnetic field, atmosphere, and climate of Mars.

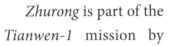

Space Fact: *Opportunity* sent back more than 342,000 photos of Mars.

Weapons in Space

While space is generally seen as a place for exploration and discovery, it can also lead to conflict and competition. Since the dawn of the space age, humans have been developing and testing various weapons in space, for both defensive and offensive purposes. Some of these weapons are real and operational, while others are still in development.

During the Cold War, the United States and the Soviet Union were engaged in a nuclear arms race, and both sides wanted to use space as a platform for launching or detonating nuclear weapons. In 1958, the US launched Operation Argus, which involved exploding three small nuclear bombs

X-17 Rocket with Nuclear Warhead (Operation Argus)

in orbit to create artificial radiation belts around the Earth. The purpose was to test the effects of nuclear explosions in space. The results were inconclusive, but the project raised concerns about the environmental and political consequences of nuclear weapons in space.

In 1962, the US conducted another nuclear test in space, called Starfish Prime. This time, a 1.4 megaton bomb was detonated at an altitude of 400 kilometers, creating a huge fireball and a bright aurora

Starfish Prime Aurora from Honolulu

that could be seen from Hawaii to New Zealand. The explosion also damaged or destroyed several satellites in orbit, including *Telstar 1*, the first commercial communications satellite. The test showed that nuclear weapons in space could have devastating effects.

In response to these tests, the international community agreed to ban nuclear weapons in space by signing the Outer Space Treaty in 1967. The treaty declared that space should be used for peaceful purposes only, and prohibited the placement of nuclear weapons or other weapons of mass destruction in orbit or on celestial bodies. The treaty also established the principle of free access and exploration of space for all nations.

However, the treaty did not prevent the development of other types of weapons in space, such as anti-satellite weapons (ASATs), ballistic missile defense systems (BMDs), or directed-energy weapons (DEWs). These weapons are designed to attack or defend against targets in space or on Earth, using kinetic energy, lasers, microwaves, or other means.

In 2019, the United States created the Space Force, a new branch of the military that will operate in space. China also has a space force, and it is likely that more countries will establish their own in the coming years.

UNITED STATES
SPACE FORCE

The Space Force Logo

The future of weapons in space is uncertain and unpredictable. Some experts believe that space will become more militarized and weaponized as more countries and actors enter the space domain and compete for resources and influence. Others hope that space will remain peaceful and cooperative as more countries and actors realize the benefits and challenges of sharing and preserving the common heritage of mankind.

Space Fact: The budget of America's Space Force is over $15 billion.

Private Space Exploration

For a long time, only governments had the money and the technology to send rockets and spacecraft into space. They used space for scientific research, military purposes, and national pride. But in the twenty-first century, things started to change. A new wave of private companies emerged that wanted to make space more accessible and affordable for everyone. They had different goals and visions, but they all shared a passion for space exploration.

One of these companies is SpaceX, founded by Elon Musk in 2002. Elon Musk is a billionaire entrepreneur who also created PayPal, Tesla,

Elon Musk

SpaceX Logo

and Neuralink. He is famous for his ambitious and visionary ideas, such as colonizing Mars, creating a global internet network with satellites, and developing a brain-computer interface. He believes that humanity needs to become a multi-planetary species to survive and thrive in the future.

SpaceX's mission is to revolutionize space technology and enable people to live on other planets. To achieve this, it designs, manufactures, and launches advanced rockets and spacecraft that can carry cargo and crew to orbit and beyond. Some of the products that SpaceX has developed are *Falcon 9*, *Falcon Heavy*, *Dragon*, *Starship*, and Starlink.

Falcon 9 is a reusable rocket that can launch satellites and spacecraft into orbit. It can land back on Earth after each mission, saving money and

Falcon 9

resources. *Falcon Heavy* is a bigger version of *Falcon 9* that can lift heavier payloads into orbit or deep space. It is one of the most powerful operational rockets in the world. *Dragon* is a spacecraft that can carry cargo and crew to the ISS and other destinations in orbit. It can also return to Earth with scientific experiments and other materials. *Starship* is a fully reusable, super heavy-lift launch system that can carry up to 100 people or tons of cargo to the Moon, Mars, or other planets. It consists of a giant rocket booster called *Super Heavy* and a spaceship called *Starship*. It

Falcon Heavy

Dragon

Starship

is still in development and testing. Starlink is a constellation of thousands of small satellites that provide high-speed internet access to anywhere on Earth. It aims to connect people who are underserved by traditional internet providers.

SpaceX has achieved many remarkable feats in its history. It is the first private company to launch a liquid-fueled

Falcon 1

rocket into orbit (*Falcon 1* in 2008), the first to launch, orbit, and recover a spacecraft (*Dragon* in 2010), the first to send a spacecraft to the ISS (*Dragon* in 2012), the first to land an orbital rocket booster on land or at sea (*Falcon 9* in 2015), and the first to reuse an orbital rocket booster (*Falcon 9* in 2017).

SpaceX is not the only private company that is involved in space exploration. There are others, such as Blue Origin, Virgin Galactic,

Orbital Sciences Corporation, Sierra Nevada Corporation, Boeing, Lockheed Martin, and many more. They have different approaches and strategies, but they all contribute to the advancement of space technology and the expansion of human presence in space.

Space Fact: The cost of a SpaceX launch is 10 times cheaper than what NASA launches used to cost.

The New Space Race

The first space race between the US and the USSR ended with the collapse of the Soviet Union in 1991, but in the twenty-first century, a new space race has emerged, involving not only the United States and Russia, but also other countries and actors. Some of the new players in the new space race are China, India, Japan, Europe, Israel, Iran, North Korea, and private companies.

China has been rapidly developing its space program since the 1990s, with the aim of becoming a major space power. China has launched several satellites, probes, rovers, and spacecraft into orbit and beyond. China has also sent humans into space and built its own space station. China's ultimate goal is to land humans on the Moon and eventually on Mars.

One of the main reasons for China's interest in space is to compete with the US, which has been the dominant space power for decades. The US has also been pursuing ambitious space projects, such as the Artemis program, which aims to return humans to the Moon by the mid-2020s and to eventually

Artemis Program Logo

establish a permanent lunar base. The US also plans to send humans to Mars in the 2030s, using the Moon as a stepping stone. The US has also been collaborating with other countries and private companies, such as SpaceX and Blue Origin, to develop reusable rockets and commercial space flights.

The new space race is not only about discovery, but also about politics, economics, and security. Space exploration offers many benefits, such as scientific knowledge, technological innovation, communication, navigation, weather forecasting, and Earth observation. Space is also a strategic region that can be used for military purposes, such as intelligence, surveillance, and missile defense. However, space is also a challenging and risky environment that poses many dangers, such as orbital debris, radiation, collisions, and cyberattacks.

The new space race is an exciting and important phenomenon that will shape the future of humanity. It will also test the limits of human ingenuity, courage, and cooperation. The new space race is not only a competition, but also an opportunity for collaboration and dialogue among different nations and actors.

Space Fact: The four countries that have so far landed on the moon are the United States, Russia, China, and India.

The Future of Space Exploration

Thanks to new technology, wealth, and know-how, the human race's ability to explore space is growing day by day.

NASA plans to send humans to Mars in the 2030s. The journey will take about six months each way. The astronauts will have to live and work on Mars for at least a year before returning to Earth. They will face many challenges and dangers, such as radiation, dust storms, isolation, and low gravity. They will also have to grow their own food and recycle their water and waste. But they will also have the opportunity to make history and discover new things about Mars and themselves.

Another goal of space exploration is to establish a permanent presence on the Moon. The Moon is closer and easier to reach than Mars, as it takes only about three days to travel there from Earth. It will be used not only to test technology, tools, and instruments that will be needed for Mars, but it may be possible to produce rocket fuel for the long trip to the Red Planet there.

NASA plans to send humans back to the Moon in the mid-2020s. The last time humans walked on the Moon was in 1972. The new program is called Artemis, after the Greek goddess of the Moon and the twin sister of Apollo, the name of the previous lunar program. NASA will use a new rocket called the *Space Launch System* (SLS) and a new spacecraft called *Orion* to carry astronauts to the Moon. NASA will also build a small space station called Gateway in orbit around the Moon. Gateway will serve as a stopover point for lunar missions and a starting point for deeper space exploration.

Space Launch System

Orion

Gateway

One of the benefits of space exploration is that it can provide valuable resources for humanity. Some of these resources include minerals, metals, water, and energy. For example, some asteroids are rich in metals, such as iron, nickel, gold, and platinum. These could be mined and used for various purposes on Earth or in space. Ice can also be found on some asteroids and comets. Water can be used for drinking, farming, or making rocket fuel by splitting it into hydrogen and oxygen.

Several private companies are interested in asteroid mining and have plans to launch missions in the near future. These aim to identify and extract resources from near-Earth asteroids using robotic spacecraft.

One of the dreams of space exploration is to travel beyond our solar system and visit other stars and planets. This is called interstellar travel, and it is very difficult and expensive to achieve. The nearest star to our Sun is Proxima Centauri, which is about 4 light-years away. To travel this distance with current technology would take thousands of years.

However, some scientists and engineers are working on new ways to make interstellar travel possible in the future. One of these projects is Breakthrough Starshot, which aims to send tiny spacecraft called *StarChips* to Proxima Centauri using powerful lasers. The *StarChips* would be attached to thin sails that would catch the laser beams and accelerate them to 20 percent of the speed of light. At this speed, they could reach Proxima Centauri in about 20 years.

Space exploration is an amazing adventure that can expand our knowledge, imagination, and horizons. It can also help us solve some of the problems we face on Earth, such as climate change, resource scarcity, and overpopulation. By exploring space, we can learn more about ourselves and our place in the universe.

Word List

A

- [ ] **A.D.** 略 キリスト紀元[西暦]〜年 《ラテン語 Anno Domini（= in the year of our Lord）の略》
- [ ] **ability** 名 ①できること，（〜する）能力 ②才能
- [ ] **aboard** 副 船[列車・飛行機・バス]に乗って
- [ ] **absorb** 動 吸収する
- [ ] **accelerate** 動 加速する
- [ ] **accelerating** 形 加速させる
- [ ] **access** 名 ①接近，近づく方法，通路 ②（システムなどへの）アクセス free access 自由なアクセス internet access インターネット・アクセス[接続]
- [ ] **accessible** 形 近づきやすい，利用できる
- [ ] **accident** 名 （不慮の）事故，災難
- [ ] **accompany** 動 ついていく，つきそう
- [ ] **according to** 〜によれば[よると]
- [ ] **accuracy** 名 正確さ，精度，的確さ
- [ ] **achieve** 動 成し遂げる，達成する
- [ ] **achievement** 名 ①達成，成就 ②業績
- [ ] **acid** 名 酸
- [ ] **active** 形 ①活動的な ②積極的な ③活動[作動]中の
- [ ] **actor** 名 （国家以外の）行為者
- [ ] **actually** 副 実際に，本当に，実は
- [ ] **add** 動 加える，足す
- [ ] **addition** 名 付加，追加，添加 ②足し in addition 加えて，さらに
- [ ] **advanced** 形 上級の，先に進んだ，高等の
- [ ] **advancement** 名 進歩，前進，昇進
- [ ] **advantage** 名 有利な点[立場]，強み，優越
- [ ] **adventure** 名 冒険
- [ ] **affect** 動 影響する
- [ ] **affordable** 形 手ごろな[良心的な]価格の
- [ ] **Africa** 名 アフリカ《大陸》
- [ ] **after** 接 after that その後 name after 〜にちなんで名付ける
- [ ] **age of** 〜の時代
- [ ] **Age of Discovery** 発見時代（大航海時代）《15世紀半ばから17世紀半ばまでのヨーロッパ人による航海

や探検が行われた時代》

- ☐ **Age of Exploration** 大航海時代《15世紀半ばから17世紀半ばまでのヨーロッパ人による航海や探検が行われた時代》

- ☐ **agency** 名 機関, 政府機関 space agency 宇宙機関

- ☐ **ago** 熟 long ago ずっと前に, 昔

- ☐ **agriculture** 名 農業, 農耕

- ☐ **aim** 動 ねらう, 目指す 名 ねらい, 目標 with the aim of ~を目的として, ~のために

- ☐ **airplane** 名 飛行機

- ☐ **Aldrin** 名 (エドウィン・"バズ"・)オルドリン《アメリカ航空宇宙局(NASA)の宇宙飛行士, 1930–》

- ☐ **all** 熟 all over ~中で, 全体に亘って, ~の至る所で first of all まず第一に

- ☐ **allow** 動 ①許す, 《 – … to ~》…が~するのを可能にする, …に~させておく ②与える

- ☐ **along the way** 途中で, これまでに, この先

- ☐ **also** 熟 not only ~ but also … ~だけでなく…もまた

- ☐ **alter** 動 (部分的に)変える, 変わる

- ☐ **although** 接 ~だけれども, ~にもかかわらず, たとえ~でも

- ☐ **altitude** 名 高度, 標高

- ☐ **amazing** 形 驚くべき, 見事な

- ☐ **amazingly** 副 驚くほどに

- ☐ **ambition** 名 大望, 野心

- ☐ **ambitious** 形 大望のある, 野心的な

- ☐ **American** 形 アメリカ(人)の 名 アメリカ人

- ☐ **ammonia** 名 アンモニア

- ☐ **among** 熟 be popular among ~の間で人気がある

- ☐ **amount** 名 量

- ☐ **analysis** 名 分析, 解析(学)

- ☐ **analyze** 動 ①分析する, 解析する, 細かく検討する ②精神分析する ③解剖する

- ☐ **ancient** 形 昔の, 古代の

- ☐ **and so** そこで, それだから, それで

- ☐ **Andromeda Galaxy** アンドロメダ星雲

- ☐ **announce** 動 (人に)知らせる, 公表する

- ☐ **another** 熟 one another お互い

- ☐ **Antarctica** 名 南極大陸

- ☐ **antenna** 名 アンテナ

- ☐ **anti-satellite weapons (ASATs)** 衛星攻撃兵器《地球周回軌道上の人工衛星を攻撃する兵器》

- ☐ **any** 熟 than any other ほかのどの~よりも

- ☐ **anymore** 副 《通例否定文, 疑問文で》今はもう, これ以上, これから

- ☐ **anywhere** 副 どこかへ[に], どこにも, どこへも, どこにでも

- ☐ **apart** 副 ①ばらばらに, 離れて ②別にして, それだけで

- ☐ **Apollo** 名 アポロ《美・詩・音楽の神, ギリシャ神話》

- ☐ **Apollo 1** アポロ1号《最初の有人宇宙飛行計画。打ち上げの予行演習中に火災事故が発生し3人の飛行士が死亡。1967年》

- ☐ **Apollo 7** アポロ7号《アポロ計画で初めての有人宇宙飛行を行なった。1968年》

- ☐ **Apollo 8** アポロ8号《アポロ計画における2度目の有人宇宙飛行。地球周回軌道を離れて月を周回し, 再び安全に地球に戻ってきた初の宇宙船となった。1968年》

- ☐ **Apollo 11** アポロ11号《史上初めて人類による月面着陸に成功したアポロ宇宙船, およびそのミッションの名称。1969年》

- ☐ **Apollo 17** アポロ17号《アポロ計

A
B
C
D
E
F
G
H
I
J
K
L
M
N
O
P
Q
R
S
T
U
V
W
X
Y
Z

画における最後の飛行。1972 年》

☐ **Apollo astronauts** アポロ宇宙船の宇宙飛行士

☐ **Apollo missions** アポロ計画《アメリカ航空宇宙局（NASA）による人類初の月への有人宇宙飛行計画。1961-1975 年》

☐ **Apollo program** アポロ計画《アメリカ航空宇宙局（NASA）による人類初の月への有人宇宙飛行計画。1961-1975 年》

☐ **appear** 動（〜のように）見える
appear to するように見える

☐ **appearance** 名外見, 印象

☐ **approach** 動接近する 名接近, （〜へ）近づく道

☐ **arise** 動起こる, 発生する, 生じる

☐ **arisen** 動 arise（起こる）の過去分詞

☐ **Armstrong** （ニール・）アームストロング《アメリカ合衆国の宇宙飛行士。人類で初めて月面に降り立った。1930-2012 年》

☐ **around** 熟 go around（〜を）周回する move around あちこち移動する move around 動き回る, 〜をあちこち動かす swirl around 渦巻く

☐ **Artemis** 名アルテミス《ギリシア神話に登場する狩猟・貞潔の女神》

☐ **Artemis program** アルテミス計画《アメリカ合衆国連邦政府が出資する有人宇宙飛行（月面着陸）計画。2017 年-》

☐ **artificial object** 人工物体

☐ **artificial radiation belt** 人工放射線帯《高高度の核爆発によって作られる放射線帯》

☐ **artificial satellite** 人工衛星

☐ **as** 熟 as a result of 〜の結果（として） as many as 〜もの数の as time passed 時がたつにつれて be known as 〜として知られている be seen as 〜として見られる just as （ちょうど）であろうとおり see

〜 as … 〜を…と見る such as たとえば〜, 〜のような the same 〜 as ……と同じ（ような） 〜 times as … as A A の〜倍の…

☐ **Asia** 名アジア

☐ **aspect** 名 ①状況, 局面, 側面 ②外観, 様子

☐ **asteroid** 名小惑星

☐ **asteroid belt** 小惑星帯《小惑星が密集している火星軌道と木星軌道の間の領域》

☐ **astonishing** 形驚くべき

☐ **astronaut** 名宇宙飛行士

☐ **astronomer** 名天文学者

☐ **astronomy** 名天文学

☐ **at a distance of** 〜の距離で

☐ **at a time** 一度に

☐ **at least** 少なくとも

☐ **at this time** 現時点では, このとき

☐ **Atlantic Ocean** 大西洋

☐ **atmosphere** 名大気, 空気

☐ **atom** 名原子

☐ **attach** 動 ①取り付ける, 添える ②付随する, 帰属する

☐ **attack** 動襲う, 攻める 名攻撃

☐ **attempt** 動試みる, 企てる

☐ **attention** 名 ①注意, 集中 ②配慮, 手当て, 世話

☐ **attract** 動引きつける, 引く

☐ **aurora** 名オーロラ

☐ **avoid** 動避ける, （〜を）しないようにする

☐ **awareness** 名認識, 自覚, 意識性, 気づいていること

☐ **away** 熟 far away 遠く離れて move away from 〜から遠ざかる

☐ **axis** 名軸, 中心線

Word List

B

- **Babylonian** 名 バビロニア人
- **back** 熟 bring back 持ち帰る
- **backward** 形 後方(へ)の, 逆の
- **bacteria** 名 バクテリア, 細菌
- **ballistic missile defense systems (BMDs)** 弾道ミサイル防衛システム《弾道ミサイルからある特定の区域を防衛すること及びその構想》
- **balloon** 名 風船, 気球
- **bamboo** 形 竹の
- **ban** 動 禁止する
- **band** 名 帯
- **bare** 形 裸の, むき出しの
- **barren** 形 不毛の
- **barrier** 名 さく, 防壁, 障害(物), 障壁
- **basalt** 名 玄武岩
- **base** 名 基地, ベース
- **basic** 形 基礎の, 基本の
- **battery** 名 電池, バッテリー
- **beach ball** ビーチボール
- **beam** 名 ①長い角材, 梁 ②光線 ③輝き 動 (光などを)発する beam back (特に指向性アンテナで)送り返す
- **bear** 動 持つ, 有する
- **beauty** 名 美
- **because of** ~のために, ~の理由で
- **beginning** 名 初め, 始まり
- **behave** 動 振る舞う
- **behavior** 名 振る舞い, 態度, 行動
- **behind** 前 ①~の後ろに, ~の背後に ②~に遅れて, ~に劣って 副 ①後ろに, 背後に ②遅れて, 劣って leave behind あとにする, ~を置き去りにする
- **belief** 名 信じること, 信念, 信用

- **belong to** ~に属する
- **below** 前 ①~より下に ②~以下の, ~より劣る 副 下に[へ]
- **bend** 動 曲がる, 曲げる
- **beneath** 前 ~の下に[の], ~より低い
- **benefit** 名 利益, 恩恵
- **bent** 形 曲がった get bent 屈折する
- **beyond** 前 ~を越えて, ~の向こうに 副 向こうに
- **Big Bang** (宇宙爆発起源論の)大爆発, ビッグバン.
- **billion** 形 10億の, ばく大な, 無数の 名 10億
- **billionaire** 名 億万長者
- **biology** 名 生物学
- **birth** 名 出産, 誕生 give birth to ~を生む
- **bit** 名 小片, 細片
- **black dwarf** 黒色矮星《白色矮星が冷えて電磁波による観測が不可能となった天体》
- **black hole** ブラックホール《極めて高密度で, 極端に重力が強いために物質だけでなく光さえ脱出することができない天体》
- **blanket** 名 毛布
- **blaze** 動 燃え立つ, かっとする
- **blazing** 形 赤々と燃え上がる
- **blob** 名 小さなかたまり
- **blow** 動 ①(風が)吹く, (風が)~を吹き飛ばす ②破裂する blow up 破裂する[させる]
- **blown** 動 blow (吹く)の過去分詞
- **Blue Origin** ブルーオリジン《Amazon.comの設立者であるジェフ・ベゾスが設立した航空宇宙企業》
- **board** 名 板 on board (乗り物などに)乗って, 搭乗して
- **boast** 動 自慢する, 誇る, 鼻にかける

137

□ **Boeing** 名 ボーイング《アメリカ合衆国のイリノイ州シカゴに本社を置く世界最大の航空宇宙機器開発製造会社》

□ **bold** 形 ①勇敢な, 大胆な, 奔放な ②ずうずうしい ③派手な

□ **bomb** 名 爆弾, 爆発物

□ **bone** 名 骨,《-s》骨格

□ **booster** 名 (宇宙船などの) ブースター, 補助推進ロケット

□ **border** 名 境界, へり, 国境

□ **bound** 動 ①bind (縛る, 結びつける)の過去, 過去分詞 名 境界(線), 限界

□ **brain-computer interface** ブレイン・コンピューター・インターフェース《脳をコンピューターとつなぎ, 人間の能力を高めたり, 活動を補助したりする。そのための仕組み》

□ **branch** 名 ①枝 ②支流, 支部

□ **brave** 形 勇敢な 動 勇敢に立ち向かう

□ **breakthrough** 名 突破, 打開, ブレークスルー

□ **Breakthrough Starshot** ブレークスルー・スターショット《レーザー推進式の恒星間探査機の概念実証のための機体を開発する研究および実用化計画》

□ **breathable** 形 呼吸に適した

□ **breathe** 動 呼吸する

□ **brightly** 副 明るく, 輝いて, 快活に

□ **brightness** 名 明るさ, 輝き

□ **brilliant** 形 光り輝く, 見事な, すばらしい, (知性または才能の点で)目ざましい, 才気のある。

□ **bring back** 持ち帰る

□ **broadcast** 動 放送する, 広める

□ **budget** 名 ①経費 ②予算

□ **building block** (物質の)構成要素[単位], 成分

□ **burst** 名 ①破裂, 爆発 ②突発

□ **but** 熟 not only ~ but also … ~だけでなく…もまた not ~ but … ~ではなくて… nothing but ただ~だけ, ~にすぎない, ~のほかは何も…ない

C

□ **calculate** 動 ①計算する, 算出する ②見積もる, 予想する

□ **camera** 名 カメラ

□ **Canada** 名 カナダ《国名》

□ **canned** 形 缶詰にされた

□ **capable** 形 ①《be – of ~ [~ing]》~の能力[資質]がある ②有能な

□ **capsule** 名 カプセル

□ **capture** 動 捕える

□ **carbon** 名 炭素

□ **carbon dioxide** 二酸化炭素

□ **carbon monoxide** 一酸化炭素

□ **cargo** 名 積み荷

□ **carry on** 続ける

□ **Cassini** 名 カッシーニ《アメリカ航空宇宙局 (NASA) と欧州宇宙機関 (ESA) によって開発され, 1997年に打上げられた土星探査機》

□ **cast** 動 (光・影などを)〔~に〕投げかける, 落とす

□ **celebrate** 動 祝う, 祝福する

□ **celestial** 形 天の, 空の, 天体の

□ **celestial body** 天体

□ **cell phone** 携帯電話

□ **Celsius** 形 セ氏の

□ **centimeter** 名 センチメートル《長さの単位》

□ **ceremony** 名 儀式, 式典

□ **Ceres** 名 ケレス《火星と木星の間の小惑星帯 (メインベルト) に位置する準惑星》

□ **chain reaction** 連鎖反応

Word List

□ **challenge** 图 ①挑戦 ②難関

□ **Challenger Disaster** チャレンジャー号爆発事故《1986年1月28日, アメリカ合衆国のスペースシャトルチャレンジャーが打ち上げから73秒後に分解し, 7名の乗組員が全員死亡した事故》

□ **challenging** 形 能力が試される, やる気をそそる

□ **chaos** 图 無秩序, 混乱状態

□ **character** 图 ①特性, 個性 ②(小説・劇などの) 登場人物

□ **characteristic** 图 特徴, 特性, 特色, 持ち味

□ **charged** 形 電気を帯びた

□ **Charles Lindbergh** チャールズ・リンドバーグ《アメリカ合衆国の飛行家。1927年, 大西洋単独無着陸飛行に初めて成功。1902-1974年》

□ **Charon** 图 カロン《冥王星の第1衛星かつ冥王星最大の衛星》

□ **cheering** 形 かっさいする

□ **chemistry** 图 化学, 化学的性質, 化学反応

□ **China** 图 中国《国名》

□ **Chinese** 形 中国(人)の 图 ①中国人 ②中国語

□ **circle** 動 回る, 囲む

□ **city-sized** 形 都市サイズ (数キロメートル程度) の

□ **civilization** 图 文明, 文明人(化)

□ **classify** 動 分類する, 区別する

□ **clear** 動 ①はっきりさせる ②片づける, 取り除く

□ **cliff** 图 断崖, 絶壁

□ **climate** 图 気候, 風土, 環境

□ **cloak** 图 マント, 袖なし外とう

□ **close to** 《be-》~に近い

□ **close-up** 形 近接の, クローズアップの

□ **cloud-covered** 形 雲におおわれた

□ **clump togeger** 凝集する, ひとまとまりになる

□ **cluster** 图 (密集した動物の) 群れ, 一団

□ **cm** 略 センチメートル

□ **CNSA** 略 中国国家航天局 (China National Space Administration)《中華人民共和国の国家行政機関の一つで, 同国の民用宇宙開発を管轄する機関》

□ **Cold War** 冷戦《第二次世界大戦後の世界を二分した西側諸国と, 東側諸国との対立構造》

□ **coldness** 图 寒さ

□ **collaborate** 動 共同して働く, 協力する

□ **collaboration** 图 協力, 協同

□ **collapse** 動 崩壊する, 崩れる, 失敗する

□ **collection** 图 収集, 収蔵物

□ **collective** 形 ①集合的な, 集団的な ②共通の

□ **collide** 動 ぶつかる, 衝突する

□ **Collins** 图 (マイケル・) コリンズ《アメリカ航空宇宙局 (NASA) の宇宙飛行士。1930-2021年》

□ **collision** 图 衝突, 不一致, あつれき

□ **colonize** 動 植民する, 入植する

□ **colorful** 形 ①カラフルな, 派手な ②生き生きとした

□ **Columbia Disaster** コロンビア号空中分解事故《2003年2月1日, アメリカ合衆国の宇宙船スペースシャトル「コロンビア号」が大気圏に再突入する際, テキサス州とルイジアナ州の上空で空中分解し, 7名の宇宙飛行士が犠牲になった事故》

□ **column** 图 (円) 柱

□ **coma** 图 コマ, 髪《彗星の頭部で核の周囲にある星雲状のもの》

□ **combine** 動 ①結合する [させる] ②連合する, 協力する

□ **come at a price** 高くつく, 相当の犠牲となる

□ **come down** 下りて来る

□ **comet** 名彗星

□ **Comet NEOWISE** ネオワイズ彗星《赤外線観測衛星 NEOWISE によって 2020 年に発見された長周期彗星》

□ **command** 名命令, 指揮(権)

□ **commercial** 形商業の, 営利的な

□ **communicate** 動①知らせる, 連絡する ②理解し合う

□ **communication** 名伝えること, 伝導, 連絡

□ **communication(s) satellite** 通信衛星

□ **communism** 名共産主義(体制)

□ **communist nation** 共産主義国

□ **community** 名団体, 共同社会, 地域社会

□ **compare** 動①比較する, 対照する ②たとえる

□ **compete** 動①競争する ②(競技に)参加する ③匹敵する

□ **competition** 名競争, 競合, コンペ

□ **complete** 動完成させる, 完了する

□ **complex** 形入り組んだ, 複雑な, 複合の

□ **compose** 動(～を)構成する, (～から)成る **composed of** (～から)成り立って, 構成されて

□ **composition** 名組織, 組成, 構成

□ **concept** 名①概念, 観念, テーマ ②(計画案などの)基本的な方向

□ **concern** 名①関心事 ②関心, 心配

□ **condense** 動濃縮する

□ **condition** 名①(健康)状態, 境遇 ②《-s》状況, 様子 ③条件

□ **conduct** 動①指導する ②実施する, 処理[処置]する

□ **confirmed** 形確認[立証]された

□ **conflict** 名①不一致, 衝突 ②争い, 対立 ③論争

□ **confront** 動①直面する, 立ち向かう ②突き合わせる, 比較する

□ **connect** 動つながる, つなぐ, 関係づける

□ **consist** 動①《- of ～》(部分・要素から)成る ②《- in ～》～に存在する, ～にある

□ **constellation** 名(類似の物などの)集まり

□ **construct** 動建設する, 組み立てる

□ **construction** 名構造, 建設, 工事, 建物

□ **contain** 動含む, 入っている

□ **contaminate** 動汚染する, 汚す

□ **contamination** 名汚染

□ **continent** 名大陸, 陸地

□ **continuously** 副連続して, 絶え間なく, 変わりなく

□ **contract** 動縮小する

□ **contribute** 動①貢献する ②寄稿する ③寄付する

□ **controversy** 名論争, 議論

□ **convert** 動変える, 転換する, 改宗させる

□ **cool down** 冷ます, 涼しくする

□ **cooperation** 名協力, 協業, 協調

□ **cooperative** 形協力的な, 協同の

□ **cope** 動うまく処理する, 対処する

□ **core** 名核心, 中心, 芯

□ **cosmic** 形宇宙の, 無限の

□ **cosmic ray** 宇宙線

□ **cosmos** 名宇宙, 秩序

□ **cost** 名値段, 費用 動(金・費用が)かかる, (～を)要する, (人に金額を)費やさせる

□ **could** 熟 If +《主語》+ could ～ できればなあ《仮定法》could have done ～だったかもしれない《仮定法》

□ **countless** 形 無数の, 数え切れない

□ **courage** 名 勇気, 度胸

□ **cover** 動 覆う, 包む, 隠す ②扱う, (～に) わたる, 及ぶ

□ **covered** ～で覆われた

□ **cozy** 形 居心地のよい

□ **cradle** 名 ①揺りかご ②発祥地

□ **crash** 動 (人・乗り物が) 衝突する, 墜落する

□ **crater** 名 隕石孔 [クレーター]

□ **create** 動 創造する, 生み出す, 引き起こす

□ **creativity** 名 創造性, 独創力

□ **credit** 動 (功績などが人にあると) 認める credit with ～で高い評価を得る

□ **crew** 名 クルー, 乗組員, 搭乗員

□ **criteria** 名 基準《criterion の複数》

□ **criticism** 名 批評, 非難, 反論, 評論

□ **crossing** 名 横断

□ **crowd** 名 群集, 雑踏, 多数, 聴衆

□ **crystal** 名 ①水晶 ②結晶

□ **curiosity** 名 ①好奇心 ②珍しい物 [存在]

□ **Curiosity** 名 キュリオシティ《NASA (アメリカ航空宇宙局) が火星探査ミッションで用いる無人探査車 (ローバー) の愛称》

□ **curious** 形 好奇心の強い, 珍しい, 奇妙な, 知りたがる

□ **current** 形 現在の, 目下の, 通用 [流通] している

□ **currently** 副 今のところ, 現在

□ **curved** 形 曲がった, 湾曲した

□ **cyberattack** 名 サイバー攻撃

□ **cycle** 名 周期, 循環

□ **Cygnus** 名 白鳥座

D

□ **Dactyl** 名 ダクティル《小惑星イダの周囲を回っている平均直径1.4kmの衛星》

□ **daily** 形 毎日の, 日常の

□ **damage** 名 損害, 損傷

□ **damaged** 形 損傷 [損害] を受けた

□ **daring** 形 大胆な, 向こう見ずな

□ **dark** 熟 get dark 暗くなる

□ **dark energy** ダークエネルギー《現代宇宙論および天文学において, 宇宙全体に浸透し, 宇宙の膨張を加速していると考えられる仮説上のエネルギー》

□ **darkness** 名 暗さ, 暗やみ

□ **data** 名 データ, 情報

□ **dawn** 名 ①夜明け ②《the –》初め, きざし

□ **day** 熟 day by day 日ごとに one day (未来の) いつか

□ **daytime** 名 昼間

□ **dazzling** 形 まばゆいばかりの

□ **deal** 動 ①分配する ②《– with [in] ～》～を扱う

□ **death** 名 ①死, 死ぬこと ②《the –》終えん, 消滅

□ **debris** 名 デブリ, (破壊された物の) 破片

□ **decade** 名 10年間

□ **declare** 動 宣言する

□ **decoration** 名 装飾, 飾りつけ

□ **deep space** 深宇宙《地球の大気圏外の宇宙空間》

□ **deeply** 副 深く, 非常に

□ **defend** 動 防ぐ, 守る, 弁護する

□ **defense** 名 防御, 守備

- [ ] **defensive** 形 防御の, 守備の
- [ ] **deflect** 屈折させる, ゆがめる, 偏向させる
- [ ] **degree** 名 (温度・角度の) 度
- [ ] **Deimos** デイモス《火星の二つの衛星の一つ》
- [ ] **democracy** 名 民主主義, 民主政治
- [ ] **dense** 形 濃い, 密集した
- [ ] **density** 名 密集, 濃度, 密度
- [ ] **depend on** ～をあてにする, ～しだいである
- [ ] **descent** 名 下り坂, 下降
- [ ] **desert** 名 砂漠, 不毛の地
- [ ] **design** 動 設計する, 企てる 名 デザイン, 設計(図)
- [ ] **despite** 前 ～にもかかわらず
- [ ] **destination** 名 行き先, 目的地
- [ ] **destroy** 動 破壊する, 絶滅させる, 無効にする
- [ ] **detail** 名 細部, 《-s》詳細
- [ ] **detect** 動 見つける
- [ ] **detector** 名 探知機, 検波器
- [ ] **detonate** 動 爆発させる
- [ ] **devastating** 形 破壊的な, 打ちひしぐ, 痛烈な
- [ ] **develop** 動 ①発達する[させる] ②開発する
- [ ] **development** 名 ①発達, 発展 ②開発
- [ ] **device** 名 ①工夫 ②案 ③装置
- [ ] **dialogue** 名 対話, 話し合い
- [ ] **diameter** 名 直径
- [ ] **diamond** 名 ダイヤモンド
- [ ] **difficulty** 名 ①むずかしさ ②難局, 支障
- [ ] **dim** 形 薄暗い **get dim** 薄暗くなる
- [ ] **dinosaur** 名 恐竜
- [ ] **dioxide** 名 二酸化物

- [ ] **directed-energy weapons (DEWs)** 指向性エネルギー兵器 《兵器操作者が意図した目標に対し指向性のエネルギーを直接に照射攻撃を行い, 目標物を破壊したり機能を停止させる兵器》
- [ ] **direction** 名 方向, 方角
- [ ] **disadvantage** 名 不利な立場[条件], 損失
- [ ] **discomfort** 名 不快(なこと), 辛苦, つらさ
- [ ] **discovery** 名 発見
- [ ] **disk** 名 円盤(状の物)
- [ ] **distance** 名 距離, 隔たり, 遠方 **at a distance of** ～の距離で
- [ ] **distant** 形 遠い, 隔たった
- [ ] **distinctive** 形 独特の, 特色[特徴]のある
- [ ] **diverse** 形 ①種々の, 多様な ②異なった
- [ ] **divide** 動 分かれる, 分ける, 割れる, 割る **be divided into** 分けられる **divide into** ～に分かれる
- [ ] **domain** 名 ①統治地域, 領土 ②領域, 分野 ③(インターネットの)ドメイン **space domain** 宇宙領域
- [ ] **dominant** 形 支配的な, 優勢な
- [ ] **dot** 名 ①点, 小数点 ②水玉(模様)
- [ ] **down** 熟 **come down** 下りて来る **cool down** 冷ます, 涼しくする
- [ ] **Dragon** 名 ドラゴン《アメリカの民間宇宙企業スペースX社により開発された無人宇宙船》
- [ ] **drama** 名 劇, 演劇, ドラマ, 劇的な事件
- [ ] **dramatic** 形 劇的な, 印象的な, 劇の
- [ ] **drawback** 名 障害, 不利, 欠点
- [ ] **dream of** ～を夢見る
- [ ] **dried** 形 乾燥した
- [ ] **drill** 名 (穴をあける)きり, ドリル
- [ ] **driven by** 《be－》～によって決

Word List

定される, 動かされる

- **drone** 图 無人機[車], ドローン
- **due** 形 予定された, 期日のきている, 支払われるべき **due to** ～によって, ～が原因で
- **dusk** 图 夕闇, 薄暗がり
- **dust** 图 ちり, ほこり, ごみ, 粉
- **dust storm** 砂塵あらし
- **dust tail** ちりの尾
- **dusty** 形 ほこりだらけの
- **dwarf** 形 矮小な
- **dwarf planet** 準惑星《太陽の周囲を公転する惑星以外の天体のうち, それ自身の重力によって球形になれるだけの質量を有するもの》

E

- **each one** 各自
- **each other** お互いに
- **Eagle** 图 月着陸船イーグル《アポロ11号で初めて人間が月面に降り立った際に使用された宇宙船》
- **earn** 動 ①儲ける, 稼ぐ ②(名声を)博す
- **earthquake** 图 地震, 大変動
- **easily** 副 容易に, たやすく, 苦もなく
- **eclipse** 图 月食, 日食
- **economic** 形 経済学の, 経済上の
- **economy** 图 経済, 財政
- **edge** 图 ①刃 ②端, 縁
- **Edwin "Buzz" Aldrin** エドウィン・"バズ"・オルドリン《アメリカ航空宇宙局(NASA)の宇宙飛行士, 1930年-》
- **Edwin Hubble** エドウィン・ハッブル《アメリカ合衆国の天文学者。1889-1953年》
- **effect** 图 影響, 効果, 結果

- **efficient** 形 効率的な, 有効な
- **effort** 图 努力(の成果)
- **electricity** 图 電気
- **electromagnetic radiation** 電磁放射線《放射線のうち電磁波であるものをいい, 一般に, 赤外線, 可視光線, 紫外線, エックス線(X線), ガンマ線(γ線)をさす》
- **elegance** 图 優雅さ, 上品さ
- **element** 图 要素, 成分, 元素
- **elliptical** 形 楕円形の
- **elliptical galaxy** 楕円銀河《渦巻き構造がなく, 楕円形に見える銀河》
- **Elon Musk** イーロン・マスク《南アフリカ共和国並びにカナダ, アメリカ合衆国国籍の起業家。PayPal, スペースX, テスラ, ボーリング・カンパニー, OpenAI, xAI等を共同設立。スペースX, テスラのCEO, X Corp.(旧: Twitter)の執行会長兼CTO。1971年-》
- **emerge** 動 現れる, 浮かび上がる, 明らかになる
- **emperor** 图 皇帝, 天皇
- **emperor penguin** コウテイペンギン
- **emptiness** 图 から, 空虚
- **enable** 動 (～することを)可能にする, 容易にする
- **encircle** (～を)(取り)囲む
- **endurance** 图 忍耐, 我慢, 耐久性
- **endure** 動 ①我慢する, 耐え忍ぶ ②持ちこたえる
- **energetic** 形 エネルギッシュな, 精力的な, 活動的な
- **engage** 動 携わる
- **engineer** 图 技師
- **engineering** 图 工学
- **enormous** 形 ばく大な, 非常に大きい, 巨大な
- **ensure** 動 確実にする, 保証する
- **entire** 形 全体の, 完全な, まったくの

- □ **entirely** 副 完全に, まったく
- □ **entrepreneur** 名 起業家
- □ **envelop** 動 包む, くるむ
- □ **envelope** 名 外皮, 包皮
- □ **environment** 名 環境
- □ **environmental** 形 環境の
- □ **equator** 名《the –》赤道
- □ **equipment** 名 装置, 機材, 道具, 設備
- □ **era** 名 時代, 年代
- □ **Eris** 名 エリス《冥王星型天体の1つに属する準惑星》
- □ **erosion** 名 浸食, 衰退
- □ **erupt** 動 (火山が)噴火する, 噴出する, 爆発する
- □ **eruption** 名 ①発生 ②爆発, 噴火
- □ **escape** 動 逃げる, 免れる, もれる
- □ **essential** 形 本質的な, 必須の
- □ **establish** 動 確立する, 立証する, 設置[設立]する
- □ **estimate** 動 ①見積もる ②評価する
- □ **Europa** 名 エウロパ《木星の第2衛星。月よりわずかに小さく, 太陽系内の衛星の中では6番目に大きい》
- □ **Europe** 名 ヨーロッパ
- □ **European** 名 ヨーロッパ人 形 ヨーロッパ(人)の
- □ **European Space Agency** 欧州宇宙機関《1975年5月30日にヨーロッパ各国が共同で設立した, 宇宙開発・研究機関である。設立参加国は当初10か国, 現在は22か国が参加》
- □ **even though** ～であるけれども, ～にもかかわらず
- □ **evening star** 宵の明星
- □ **eventually** 副 結局は
- □ **ever since** それ以来ずっと
- □ **Everest, Mt.** エベレスト山
- □ **everyday** 形 毎日の, 日々の

- □ **everyone** 代 誰でも, 皆
- □ **everything** 代 すべてのこと[もの], 何でも, 何もかも
- □ **evidence** 名 ①証拠, 証人 ②形跡
- □ **evolve** 動 進化する[させる], 発展する[させる]
- □ **example** 熟 for example たとえば
- □ **except for** ～を除いて, ～がなければ
- □ **exciting** 形 興奮させる, わくわくさせる
- □ **exercise** 動 運動する
- □ **exhaust** 名 排気, 排出
- □ **exist** 動 存在する, 生存する, ある, いる
- □ **existence** 名 存在, 実在, 生存
- □ **exoplanet** 名 太陽系外惑星, 系外惑星
- □ **expand** 動 ①広げる, 拡張[拡大]する ②発展させる, 拡充する
- □ **expansion** 名 拡大, 拡張, 展開
- □ **expect** 動 予期[予測]する, (当然のこととして)期待する
- □ **experiment** 名 実験, 試み
- □ **expert** 名 専門家, 熟練者, エキスパート
- □ **explode** 動 爆発する[させる]
- □ **exploration** 名 探検, 実地調査
- □ **explore** 動 探検[調査]する, 切り開く
- □ **explorer** 名 探検者[家]
- □ **explosion** 名 爆発, 急増
- □ **explosive** 名 爆発物, 爆薬
- □ **exposed** 形 ①雨風[光, 攻撃, 危険]にさらされた ②露出した, 無防備な ③露呈した, 覚知した
- □ **exposure** 名 ①さらされる ②暴露, 暴くこと
- □ **extract** 動 抜粋する, 抽出する
- □ **extreme** 形 極端な, 極度の, いち

144

ばん端の

□ **extremely** 副非常に，極度に

F

□ **failure** 名失敗

□ **faint** 形かすかな，弱い，ぼんやりした

□ **fairy tale** おとぎ話，童話

□ **falcon** 名ハヤブサ

□ **Falcon 1** ファルコン1《アメリカ合衆国の企業スペースX社により開発された2段式の商業用打ち上げロケット》

□ **Falcon 9** ファルコン9《アメリカ合衆国の民間企業スペースX社により開発され，打ち上げられている2段式の商業用打ち上げロケット》

□ **Falcon Heavy** ファルコンヘビー《アメリカのスペースX社が開発した宇宙飛行用の大型ロケット（打ち上げ機）》

□ **fall into** ～に陥る，～してしまう

□ **familiar** 形①親しい，親密な ②普通の，いつもの，おなじみの

□ **famous for**《be –》～で有名である

□ **far** 熟 far away 遠く離れて how far どのくらいの距離か so far 今までのところ，これまでは

□ **farther** 副もっと遠く，さらに先に 形もっと向こうの，さらに進んだ

□ **fascinating** 形魅惑的な，うっとりさせるような

□ **fascination** 名魅力，魅惑

□ **fast-moving** 形動きの速い，高速で動く

□ **feat** 名偉業，離れわざ

□ **feature** 名特徴，特色

□ **feel like** ～のような感じがする

□ **Ferdinand Magellan** フェルディナンド・マゼラン《大航海時代のポルトガル出身のスペインの航海者，探検家。1480-1521年》

□ **few** 熟 quite a few かなり多くの

□ **fiery** 形①火の，燃えさかる ②火のように赤い

□ **55 Cancri e** かに座55番星e《地球から40.25光年離れた，太陽と似た恒星かに座55番星の周りを公転する太陽系外惑星》

□ **fill in** ～に記入する

□ **final** 形最後の

□ **find out** 見つけ出す，気がつく

□ **fireball** 名火球

□ **first of all** まず第一に

□ **flat** 形平らな

□ **flatten** 動①平らにする，伸ばす ②ばったりと倒す

□ **flight** 名飛ぶこと，飛行，（飛行機の）フライト

□ **float** 動①浮く，浮かぶ ②漂流する

□ **flowing** 形流れる，流れている

□ **fly by** ～に接近飛行する

□ **focus** 名①焦点，ピント ②関心の的，着眼点 ③中心 動①焦点を合わせる ②（関心・注意を）集中させる

□ **following** 形《the –》次の，次に続く

□ **footprint** 名足型，足跡

□ **for** 熟 for a moment 少しの間 for example たとえば for instance たとえば for short 略して for sure 確かに for years 何年も

□ **force** 名力，勢い

□ **form** 名形，形式 動形づくる

□ **formation** 名①形成，編成 ②隊形，フォーメーション

□ **forth** 副前へ，外へ

□ **fragile** 形壊れやすい，もろい，傷つきやすい

□ **fragment** 名破片，断片，かけら

□ **France** 名フランス《国名》

□ **free access** 自由なアクセス

□ **freely** 副自由に, 障害なしに

□ **freezing** 形酷寒の, こごえるような

□ **frequency** 名周波数

□ **from now** 今から, これから

□ **front of** 《in – 》～の前に, ～の正面に

□ **frontier** 名①国境, 辺境, フロンティア ②《-s》最先端

□ **frozen** 形凍った

□ **fuel** 名燃料

□ **full of** 《be – 》～で一杯である

□ **fully** 副十分に, 完全に, まるまる

□ **functioning** 形機能する

□ **funding** 名①財源 ②財政支援 ③資金調達

□ **furnace** 名炉, かまど, 溶鉱炉

□ **fuse** 動(金属などを)溶かす, 溶ける

□ **fusion** 名融合

□ **future** 熟in the future 将来は

G

□ **G2-type star** スペクトル型 G2 型の主系列星《核で水素の核融合反応を起こしている主系列星。黄色矮星とも呼ばれる。太陽は G2 型の主系列星の一つ》

□ **Gagarin** 名(ユーリイ・)ガガーリン《ソビエト連邦の軍人, パイロット, 宇宙飛行士。人類初の有人宇宙飛行としてボストーク1号に単身搭乗した。1934–1968 年》

□ **gain** 動①得る, 増す ②進歩する, 進む

□ **galactic** 形銀河(系)の

□ **galaxy** 名①《the – , the G-》星雲, 銀河 ②《the G-》銀河系 **elliptical galaxy** 楕円銀河《渦巻き構造がなく, 楕円形に見える銀河》 **irregular galaxy** 不規則銀河《回転対称な円盤や渦巻腕を持たず, 光の集中した中心核を明確に持たない銀河》 **spiral galaxy** 渦巻銀河《恒星が密集した丸い中心核から渦巻状の腕が出て(腕の先がさらに枝分かれするものも多い)いる銀河》

□ **galaxy cluster** 銀河団《数百個から数千個の銀河が互いの重力の影響によって集団となったもの》

□ **Gale** 名ゲール《火星のクレーター》

□ **Galileo** 名①ガリレオ《1989 年 10 月 18 日にアメリカ航空宇宙局(NASA)が打ち上げた木星探査機》②ガリレオ(・ガリレイ)》

□ **Galileo Galilei** ガリレオ・ガリレイ《イタリアの自然哲学者, 天文学者, 数学者。1564–1642 年》

□ **gamma ray** ガンマ線《放射線の一種で, 波長が 10pm (0.00000001mm) 以下の電磁波》

□ **Ganymede** 名ガニメデ《木星の第3衛星。太陽系に存在する衛星の中で半径, 質量ともに最大》

□ **gas** 名ガス, 気体

□ **gas cloud** ガス雲

□ **gas tail** (彗星の)ガスの尾

□ **gaseous** 形ガス(状)の

□ **Gateway** 月軌道プラットフォームゲートウェイ《多国間で月周回軌道上に建設することが提案されている有人の宇宙ステーション》

□ **gather** 動①集まる, 集める ②生じる, 増す

□ **gaze** 動凝視する

□ **gem** 名宝石, 宝玉, すばらしいもの

□ **generally** 副①一般に, だいたい ②たいてい

□ **geology** 名地質学

□ **geostationary orbit (GEO)** 静止軌道《地球の自転周期と衛星の公転周期が一致している軌道。赤道上空約3万6000kmの軌道で, 地上からは

常に静止しているように見える》

☐ **Germany** 图ドイツ《国名》

☐ **get bent** 屈折する

☐ **get dark** 暗くなる

☐ **get dim** 薄暗くなる

☐ **get stuck in** ～にはまり込む

☐ **giant** 图巨人, 大男 形巨大な, 偉大な

☐ **gigantic** 形巨大な, 膨大な

☐ **give birth to** ～を生む

☐ **give off** 発散する, 放つ

☐ **give rise to** ～を生じさせる

☐ **Gliese 876 d** グリーゼ876d《太陽系から約15光年離れた, 赤色矮星グリーゼ876の周囲を公転する太陽系外惑星》

☐ **glimpse** 图ちらりと見ること

☐ **global** 形地球(上)の, 地球規模の, 世界的な, 国際的な

☐ **Global Positioning System (GPS)** グローバル・ポジショニング・システム《地球全体をカバーする位置測位システム》

☐ **global warming** 地球温暖化

☐ **glow** 動(火が)白熱して輝く 图白熱, 輝き

☐ **glowing** 形白熱[赤熱]した, 熱のこもった

☐ **go around** (～を)周回する

☐ **goddess** 图女神

☐ **gold** 图金

☐ **golden** 形金色の

☐ **Goldilocks and the Three Bears** 『3びきのくま』《ゴルディロックスという小さな女の子が3匹の熊に出くわす物語。ロバート・サウジー著》

☐ **Goldilocks zone** ゴルディロックス・ゾーン《宇宙において生命の進化に適した領域のこと》

☐ **golf cart** ゴルフ・カート《ゴルフ

ァーとそのゴルフクラブをゴルフコース内を歩くよりも少ない労力で運ぶために設計された小型の電動車両》

☐ **government** 图政治, 政府, 支配

☐ **GPS** 略グローバル・ポジショニング・システム (Global Positioning System)《地球全体をカバーする位置測位システム》

☐ **grab** 動①ふいにつかむ, ひったくる ②横取りする

☐ **gradually** 副だんだんと

☐ **grain** 图粒

☐ **grandeur** 图壮大さ, 雄大さ

☐ **gravitational** 形重力の, 引力の

☐ **gravitationally** 副重力[引力](の作用)で

☐ **gravity** 图重力, 引力

☐ **Great Bear** おおぐま座

☐ **Great Dark Spot** (海王星の)大暗班《海王星において見られた暗い楕円形の部分》

☐ **Great Red Spot** (木星の)大赤斑《木星の南半球にある巨大な大気渦》

☐ **greatly** 副大いに

☐ **Greek** 形ギリシア(人・語)の 图①ギリシア人 ②ギリシア語

☐ **greenhouse effect** 温室効果

☐ **greet** 動①あいさつする ②(喜んで)迎える

☐ **grip** 图①つかむこと, 把握, グリップ ②支配(力)

☐ **ground** 熟 on the ground 地面に

☐ **ground-based telescope** 地上望遠鏡

☐ **growing** 形成長期にある, 大きくなりつつある

☐ **guideline** 图ガイドライン, 指針

☐ **gunpowder** 图火薬

A
B
C
D
E
F
G
H
I
J
K
L
M
N
O
P
Q
R
S
T
U
V
W
X
Y
Z

H

□ **habitability** 名 居住適性

□ **habitable** 形 住むことができる，住むのに適した．

□ **halfway** 形 中間［中途］の

□ **Halley's Comet** ハレー彗星 《75.32 年周期で地球に接近する短周期彗星。地球から肉眼で簡単に観測可能で，多くの周期彗星の中で最初に知られた彗星》

□ **hand** 熟 on the other hand 一方，他方では

□ **Hans Lipperhey** ハンス・リッペルハイ《オランダのレンズ製作者で望遠鏡を最初に造ったとされる一人。1570–1616 年》

□ **harmful** 形 害を及ぼす，有害な

□ **harsh** 形 厳しい，とげとげしい，不快な

□ **harshness** 名 厳しさ

□ **hatch** 名 （船などの）昇降口，出入り口，ハッチ

□ **Haumea** 名 ハウメア《準惑星であり，太陽系外縁天体のサブグループである冥王星型天体の1つ》

□ **have** 熟 could have done 〜だったかもしれない《仮定法》

□ **Hawaii** 名 ハワイ《米国の州》

□ **Hayabusa** 名 はやぶさ《2003 年 5 月 9 日に宇宙科学研究所（ISAS）が打ち上げた小惑星探査機。2005 年夏に小惑星イトカワに到達し，地球重力圏外にある天体の固体表面に着陸してのサンプルリターンに世界で初めて成功した》

□ **hazardous** 形 危険な

□ **HD 189733 b** HD 189733 b《地球からこぎつね座の方向に約64.5光年離れた位置にある太陽系外惑星。木星よりわずかに大きい質量を持ち，わずか2.2日周期で軌道を公転しているホット・ジュピター》

□ **healthy** 形 健康な，健全な，健康に

よい

□ **heart-shaped** 形 ハート型の［をした］

□ **heat** 名 熱，暑さ 動 熱する，暖める

□ **heaven** 名 天，天空

□ **heavy-lift** 形 ヘビーリフト［重量物運搬］

□ **height** 名 高さ

□ **helicopter** 名 ヘリコプター

□ **helium** 名 ヘリウム

□ **help 〜 with ...** 〜に役立つ

□ **hemisphere** 名 半球（体）

□ **heritage** 名 遺産，相続財産

□ **hidden** 形 隠れた，秘密の

□ **hide** 動 隠れる，隠す，隠れて見えない，秘密にする

□ **high-speed** 形 高速度の

□ **highway** 名 幹線道路，ハイウェー，本道

□ **Hitler** 名 （アドルフ・）ヒトラー《ドイツの政治家。ドイツ国首相，および国家元首（総統）であり，国家と一体であるとされた国民社会主義ドイツ労働者党（ナチス）の指導者。1889–1945 年》

□ **hobby** 名 趣味，得意なこと

□ **honor** 動 尊敬する，栄誉を与える

□ **hoop** 名 輪，（樽などの）たが

□ **hopeful** 形 希望に満ちた，望みを抱いて（いる），有望な

□ **horizon** 名 水平線，地平線

□ **horrible** 形 恐ろしい，ひどい

□ **hostile** 形 敵意をもった，敵の

□ **hot Jupiter** ホット・ジュピター《木星ほどの質量を持つガス惑星でありながら，主星の恒星からわずかしか離れておらず，表面温度が非常に高温になっている太陽系外惑星の分類の一つ》

□ **hot spring** 温泉

□ **Houston** 名 ヒューストン《米国テ

キサス州最大の都市。NASA（米国航空宇宙局）の施設がある》

□ **how far** どのくらいの距離か

□ **how to** ～する方法

□ **however** 接 たとえ～でも 接 けれども, だが

□ **HST** 略 ハッブル宇宙望遠鏡（Hubble Space Telescope）《1990年4月24日に打ち上げられた, 地上約600km上空の軌道上を周回する宇宙望遠鏡。地球の大気や天候による影響を受けないため, 地上からでは困難な高い精度での天体観測が可能》

□ **Hubble Deep Field (HDF)** ハッブル・ディープ・フィールド《ハッブル宇宙望遠鏡による一連の観測結果に基づいた, おおぐま座の非常に狭い領域の画像》

□ **Hubble Space Telescope (HST)** ハッブル宇宙望遠鏡《1990年4月24日に打ち上げられた, 地上約600km上空の軌道上を周回する宇宙望遠鏡。地球の大気や天候による影響を受けないため, 地上からでは困難な高い精度での天体観測が可能》

□ **hue** 名 ①色合い ②傾向, 特色

□ **huge** 形 巨大な, ばく大な

□ **hugely** 副 大いに, 非常に.

□ **humanity** 名 人間性, 人間らしさ

□ **human-made** 形 人工の

□ **hundreds of** 何百もの～

□ **hydrazine** 名 ヒドラジン《窒素と水素の化合物。ロケット・ジェットエンジンの燃料》

□ **hydrogen** 名 水素

I

□ **IAU** 略 国際天文学連合（International Astronomical Union）《世界の天文学者で構成されている国際組織。恒星や惑星, 小惑星, その他の天体とその地形に対する命名権を取り扱っている》

□ **IC 1101** IC 1101《銀河系から約10億光年離れた Abell 2029銀河団の中央部にある楕円銀河またはレンズ状銀河で, 同銀河団で最も明るい銀河》

□ **icy** 形 氷の（多い）, 氷のように冷たい

□ **ideal** 形 理想的な, 申し分のない

□ **identify** 動 （本人・同一と）確認する, 見分ける

□ **if** 熟 If +《主語》+ could ～できればなあ《仮定法》wonder if ～ではないかと思う

□ **ignite** 動 火がつく［つける］, 発火する

□ **image** 名 画像, 映像

□ **imagination** 名 想像（力）, 空想

□ **imagine** 動 想像する, 心に思い描く

□ **immense** 形 巨大な, 計り知れない, すばらしい

□ **impact** 名 影響力, 反響, 効果

□ **implement** 動 ①実行する ②道具［手段］を提供する

□ **improve** 動 改善する［させる］, 進歩する

□ **in** 熟 in addition 加えて, さらに in front of ～の前に, ～の正面に in peace 平和のうちに, 安心して in the future 将来は in the middle of ～の真ん中［中ほど］に in the world 世界で in this way このようにして in time 間に合って, やがて

□ **include** 動 含む, 勘定に入れる

□ **including** 前 ～を含めて, 込みで

□ **inconclusive** 形 決定的でない

□ **increase** 動 増加［増強］する, 増やす, 増える

□ **increasingly** 副 ますます, だんだん

□ **incredible** 形 ①信じられない, 信用できない ②すばらしい, とてつもない

□ **incredibly** 副 信じられないほど, 途方もなく

□ **India** 名 インド《国名》

□ **inevitable** 形 避けられない, 必然的な

□ **inflate** 動 ふくらます, ふくらむ

□ **influence** 名 影響, 勢力

□ **infrared light** 赤外線, 赤外光

□ **infrared telescope** 赤外線望遠鏡《天体が発する赤外線領域の電磁波を観測するため望遠鏡。一般には反射望遠鏡が使用される》

□ **infrared wave** 赤外線波《可視光線の赤い端からマイクロ波の範囲にかけての電磁スペクトルの一部である電磁波》

□ **ingenuity** 名 発明の才, 巧妙さ, 独創性

□ **Ingenuity** 名 インジェニュイティ《NASAのマーズ2020ミッションの一環として火星で運用されている小型のロボットヘリコプター。2021年4月19日, 地球以外の惑星で航空機による最初の動力制御飛行を無事に完了》

□ **ingredient** 名 成分, 原料, 材料

□ **inhospitable** 形 荒涼たる, 生存に適さない

□ **initially** 副 初めに, 初めは

□ **inner** 形 ①内部の ②心の中の

□ **innovation** 名 ①革新, 刷新 ②新しいもの, 新考案

□ **insight** 名 洞察, 真相, 見識

□ **inspire** 動 ①奮い立たせる, 鼓舞する ②(感情などを)吹き込む ③霊感を与える

□ **instance** 名 ①例 ②場合, 事実 **for instance** たとえば

□ **instead** 副 その代わりに **instead of** 〜の代わりに, 〜をしないで

□ **instrument** 名 道具, 器具, 器械

□ **intelligence** 名 ①知能 ②情報

□ **intense** 形 強烈な, 激しい

□ **interact** 動 影響しあう, 相互に作用する

□ **interested** 形 興味を持った, 関心のある **be interested in** 〜に興味[関心]がある

□ **interesting** 形 おもしろい, 興味を起こさせる

□ **interface** 名 インターフェース

□ **interfere** 動 ①じゃまをする, 干渉する ②衝突する

□ **interference** 名 妨害, 干渉

□ **internal** 形 内部の, 国内の

□ **International Astronomical Union (IAU)** 国際天文学連合《世界の天文学者で構成されている国際組織。恒星や惑星, 小惑星, その他の天体とその地形に対する命名権を取り扱っている》

□ **International Space Station (ISS)** 国際宇宙ステーション《低軌道にあるモジュール式の宇宙ステーション。宇宙生物学, 天文学, 気象学, 物理学などの分野で科学研究を行う微小重力と宇宙環境の研究所として機能》

□ **internet access** インターネット・アクセス[接続]

□ **interstellar** 形 星間の

□ **interstellar travel** 恒星間旅行

□ **introduction** 名 紹介, 導入

□ **invent** 動 発明[考案]する

□ **invention** 名 発明(品)

□ **invisible** 形 目に見えない, 表に出ない

□ **involve** 動 ①含む, 伴う ②巻き込む, かかわらせる

□ **involved** 形 巻き込まれている, 関連する

□ **Iran** 名 イラン《国名》

□ **iron** 名 鉄

□ **iron-rich** 形 鉄に富む, 鉄の多い

□ **irregular** 形 不規則な, ふぞろいの

□ **irregular galaxy** 不規則銀河《回転対称な円盤や渦巻腕を持たず, 光の集中した中心核を明確に持たない銀河》

□ **isolation** 名 孤立, 隔離

□ **Israel** 名 イスラエル《国名》

□ **ISS** 略 国際宇宙ステーション（International Space Station）《低軌道にあるモジュール式の宇宙ステーション。宇宙生物学, 天文学, 気象学, 物理学などの分野で科学研究を行う微小重力と宇宙環境の研究所として機能》

□ **issue** 名 問題, 論点

□ **It is ～ for someone to ...** （人）が...するのは～だ

□ **Italy** 名 イタリア《国名》

□ **Itokawa** 名 イトカワ《太陽系の小惑星であり, 地球に接近する地球近傍小惑星（地球に近接する軌道を持つ天体）のうちアポロ群に属する》

□ **itself** 代 それ自体, それ自身

J

□ **jam** 名 渋滞, 雑踏 **traffic jam** 交通渋滞

□ **James Webb Space Telescope (JWST)** ジェイムズ・ウェッブ宇宙望遠鏡《アメリカ航空宇宙局（NASA）が中心となって開発を行っている赤外線観測用宇宙望遠鏡。ハッブル宇宙望遠鏡の後継機》

□ **Japan** 名 日本《国名》

□ **Japanese** 形 日本（人・語）の 名 ①日本人 ②日本語

□ **JAXA** 略 宇宙航空研究開発機構（Japan Aerospace Exploration Agency）《日本の航空宇宙開発政策を担う国立研究開発法人。本部は東京都調布市》

□ **John F. Kennedy** ジョン・F・ケネディ《アメリカ合衆国の政治家。同国第35代大統領。在任1961–1963年》

□ **journey** 名 （遠い目的地への）旅

□ **Juno** 名 ジュノー《2011年8月5日に打ち上げられたNASAの木星探査機。2016年7月5日に木星の極軌道への投入に成功》

□ **Jupiter** 名 木星

□ **just as** （ちょうど）であろうとおり

□ **JWST** 略 ジェイムズ・ウェッブ宇宙望遠鏡（James Webb Space Telescope）《アメリカ航空宇宙局（NASA）が中心となって開発を行っている赤外線観測用宇宙望遠鏡。ハッブル宇宙望遠鏡の後継機》

K

□ **Kepler 186f** ケプラー186f《地球から582光年離れた赤色矮星ケプラー186を周回する太陽系外惑星。太陽以外の恒星のハビタブルゾーン（生命が存在する可能性のある領域）内において, 初めて発見された地球に近いサイズの惑星》

□ **Kessler syndrome** ケスラーシンドローム《スペースデブリの危険性を端的に説明するシミュレーションモデル。デブリ同士の衝突によって加速度的にデブリが増えるという現象》

□ **kilogram** 名 キログラム《重量の単位》

□ **kilometer** 名 キロメートル《長さの単位》

□ **kinetic energy** 運動エネルギー

□ **km** 名 キロメートル《単位》

□ **know-how** 名 ノウハウ

□ **knowledge** 名 知識, 理解, 学問

□ **known as** 《be –》～として知られている

□ **Konstantin Tsiolkovsky** コンスタンチン・ツィオルコフスキー《ロシア帝国生まれのロケット研究者,

151

物理学者。人工衛星や宇宙船の示唆、多段式ロケット、軌道エレベータなどの考案や、宇宙旅行の可能性としてロケットで宇宙に行けることを証明した。1857-1935年》

☐ **Kosmos 954** コスモス954号《1977年9月18日に打ち上げられた、ソビエト連邦のレーダー海洋偵察衛星（RORSAT）。電力源としてウラン235を燃料とする発電用の原子炉を搭載しており、1978年1月24日11時53分にカナダ西海岸のクィーン・シャーロット島北部でカナダ領空に進入し、カナダ北西部の無人地帯に墜落》

☐ **Kuiper Belt** カイパーベルト《太陽系の海王星軌道（太陽から約30 au）より外側からおよそ50 auまでの黄道面付近にある、天体が密集した穴の空いた円盤状の領域であり、星周円盤の一種》

L

☐ **laboratory** 名実験室、研究室

☐ **lack** 動不足している、欠けている 名不足、欠乏

☐ **landing** 名上陸、着陸

☐ **landscape** 名景色、風景

☐ **laser** 名レーザー

☐ **last time** 《the – 》この前〜したとき

☐ **launch** 動（ロケットなどを）打ち上げる、発射する

☐ **laws of physics** 物理法則

☐ **layer** 名層、重ね

☐ **lead** 名鉛

☐ **lead to** 〜に至る、〜に通じる、〜を引き起こす

☐ **leak** 名もれ（口）、漏洩

☐ **leap** 名跳ぶこと

☐ **least** 名最小、最少 **at least** 少なくとも

☐ **leave behind** あとにする、〜を置き去りにする

☐ **led** 動 lead（導く）の過去、過去分詞

☐ **leftover** 名残り物

☐ **legacy** 名遺産、遺贈品

☐ **legal** 形法律（上）の、正当な

☐ **lense** 名レンズ

☐ **lie** 動（ある状態に）ある、存在する

☐ **lift** 動持ち上げる、上がる

☐ **light pollution** 光害

☐ **light-year** 名光年《光が1年間に達する距離》。

☐ **like** 熟 **feel like** 〜のような感じがする **sound like** 〜のように聞こえる

☐ **likely** 形ありそうな、もっともらしい

☐ **limit** 名限界、《-s》範囲、境界 動制限[限定]する

☐ **limitation** 名制限、限度

☐ **limited** 形限られた、限定の

☐ **liquid** 名液体 形液体（状）の

☐ **liquid-fueled rocket** 液体燃料ロケット《液体燃料と液体酸化剤を使うロケット。燃料の単位あたりの推力が高く、点火時間を調整できる》

☐ **living** 形生きている、現存の

☐ **locate** 動置く、居住する[させる]

☐ **location** 名位置、場所

☐ **Lockheed Martin** ロッキード・マーティン《アメリカ合衆国の航空機・宇宙船の開発製造会社》

☐ **long ago** ずっと前に、昔

☐ **long-ago** 形昔の

☐ **longer** 熟 **no longer** もはや〜でない[〜しない]

☐ **look for** 〜を探す

☐ **look up** 見上げる

☐ **low Earth Orbit (LEO)** 地球低軌道《地球の周囲を周回する軌道で、周期が128分以下（1日に少なくとも

11.25 周する）の軌道のこと。宇宙空間にある人工物体のほとんどは LEO にある》

□ **lunar** 形 月の, 月面の

□ **lunar module** アポロ月着陸船《アポロ計画において, 二名の宇宙飛行士を月面に着陸させ, かつ帰還させるために開発された宇宙船》

M

□ **made of** ～でできて[作られて]いる

□ **made up of** ①《be –》～で構成されている ②～で作られた, ～で構成[形成]された

□ **Magellan** マゼラン《アメリカ航空宇宙局（NASA）が1989年に打ち上げた惑星探査機。金星を探査することが目的であり, レーダーにより金星地表の地形を明らかにした》

□ **Magellanic Clouds** マゼラン雲《銀河系の近くにある2つの銀河, 大マゼラン雲と小マゼラン雲の総称》

□ **magnet** 名 磁石, 引きつけるもの

□ **magnetic field** 磁場, 磁界

□ **magnetism** 名 磁気, 磁性

□ **magnify** 動 拡大する

□ **main** 形 主な, 主要な

□ **maintain** 動 維持する

□ **majesty** 名 威厳, 壮麗さ

□ **major** 形 大きいほうの, 主な

□ **make it possible for ~ to ...** ～が…できるようにする

□ **make ~ out of ...** ～を…から作る

□ **make sure** 確かめる, 確認する

□ **Makemake** 名 マケマケ《準惑星であり, 太陽系外縁天体のサブグループである冥王星型天体の1つ》

□ **malfunction** 名 機能不全, 故障

動 正常に働かない

□ **manage** 動 動かす, うまく処理する

□ **mankind** 名 人類, 人間

□ **manned** 形 人間を乗せた

□ **manned lunar mission** 有人月探査計画

□ **manned spaceflight** 有人宇宙飛行

□ **manufacture** 動 製造[製作]する

□ **many as** 《as –》～もの数の

□ **Mariner 10** マリナー10号《1973年に打ち上げられたアメリカ航空宇宙局（NASA）の宇宙探査機。マリナー計画の最終機で, 金星および水星を探査した。人類が初めて水星を調査した探査機》

□ **mark** 動 印[記号]をつける

□ **Mars** 名 火星

□ **Mars 2020** マーズ2020《アメリカ航空宇宙局（NASA）火星探査プログラムによるミッションであり, 火星ローバー「パーサヴィアランス」と小型の火星ヘリコプター「インジェニュイティ」から構成される。2020年7月30日に打ち上げられ, 2021年2月18日に火星のジェゼロ・クレーターに着陸した》

□ **Mars Exploration Rover (MER)** マーズ・エクスプロレーション・ローバー《2003年にアメリカ航空宇宙局（NASA）が打ち上げた, 火星の表面を探査する2機の無人火星探査車》

□ **Mars rover** マーズ・ローバー, 火星探査車《火星着陸後に火星表面を自動で走行するローバー》

□ **Mars Science Laboratory (MSL)** マーズ・サイエンス・ラボラトリー《アメリカ航空宇宙局（NASA）が火星探査ミッションで用いる宇宙船の名称》

□ **marvel** 名 驚くべきもの[こと], 不

思議(なもの)

- [ ] **mass** 名 ①固まり，(密集した)集まり ②多数，多量
- [ ] **mass destruction** 大量破壊
- [ ] **massive** 形 巨大な，大量の
- [ ] **material** 名 材料，原料
- [ ] **matter** 熟 **no matter** 〜を問わず，どうでもいい
- [ ] **measure** 動 ①測る，(〜の)寸法がある ②評価する
- [ ] **mechanical** 形 機械の，機械的な
- [ ] **media** 名 メデイア，マスコミ，媒体
- [ ] **medical** 形 医学の
- [ ] **medium Earth orbit (MEO)** 中軌道《低軌道(約2,000km以下)と対地同期軌道(平均高度約36,000km)の中間に位置する人工衛星の軌道の総称》
- [ ] **medium-sized** 形 Mサイズの，中型の
- [ ] **megaton** 名 メガトン《TNT100万トンに相当する爆発力。水爆などの爆発力について用いる単位》
- [ ] **melt** 動 溶ける，溶かす
- [ ] **mention** 動 (〜について)述べる，言及する
- [ ] **Mercury** 名 水星
- [ ] **merely** 副 単に，たかが〜に過ぎない
- [ ] **merge** 動 合併する[させる]，融合する[させる]，溶け込む[ませる]
- [ ] **mesmerizing** 形 魅惑する
- [ ] **messenger** 名 使者，(伝言・小包などの)配達人，伝達者
- [ ] **metal** 名 金属，合金
- [ ] **meteor** 名 流星，隕石
- [ ] **meteorite** 名 隕石
- [ ] **meter** 名 メートル《長さの単位》
- [ ] **methane** 名 メタン
- [ ] **method** 名 方法，手段
- [ ] **Michael Collins** マイケル・コリ

ンズ《アメリカ航空宇宙局(NASA)の宇宙飛行士。1930-2021年》

- [ ] **microgravity** 名 微小重力
- [ ] **microphone** 名 マイクロフォン，マイク
- [ ] **microscope** 名 顕微鏡
- [ ] **microwave** 名 マイクロ波
- [ ] **microwave oven** 電子レンジ
- [ ] **mid** 形 中間の，中央の，中間部分の
- [ ] **middle** 名 中間，最中 **in the middle of** 〜の真ん中[中ほど]に
- [ ] **middle-aged** 形 中高年の
- [ ] **might** 助 《mayの過去》①〜かもしれない ②〜してもよい，〜できる
- [ ] **mile** 名 ①マイル《長さの単位。1,609m》②《-s》かなりの距離
- [ ] **milestone** 名 画期的出来事[事件]，節目
- [ ] **militarized** 形 軍事化する
- [ ] **military** 形 軍隊[軍人]の，軍事の 名 《the –》軍，軍部
- [ ] **Milky Way** 天の川銀河，銀河系《太陽系を含む銀河》
- [ ] **mind** 名 心
- [ ] **mine** 動 採掘する
- [ ] **mineral** 名 鉱物，鉱石
- [ ] **Miranda** 名 ミランダ《天王星の第5衛星。太陽系の中で最も極端かつ多様な地形を持つ》
- [ ] **mirror** 名 鏡
- [ ] **missile** 名 ミサイル
- [ ] **mission** 名 使命，任務
- [ ] **mist** 名 霧，もや，蒸気
- [ ] **mistook** 動 mistake(間違える)の過去
- [ ] **mitigate** 動 やわらげる，静める，鎮静する
- [ ] **mix** 動 ①混ざる，混ぜる ②(〜を)一緒にする 名 混合(物)
- [ ] **mixture** 名 ①混合 ②入り混じったもの

□ **moderate** 形穏やかな, 適度な, 手ごろな

□ **modern** 形現代［近代］の, 現代的な, 最近の

□ **module** 名基準単位, モジュール **lunar module** アポロ月着陸船《アポロ計画において, 二名の宇宙飛行士を月面に着陸させ, かつ帰還させるために開発された宇宙船》**service module** サービスモジュール《有人宇宙カプセルに付随する無人の宇宙船で, 電気システムや推進システムなどの重要なサブシステムを搭載している》

□ **molecule** 名分子, 微粒子 **organic molecule** 有機分子

□ **moment** 名①瞬間, ちょっとの間 ②(特定の) 時, 時期 **for a moment** 少しの間

□ **money** 熟 **save money** コストを削減する, 貯金する

□ **monitor** 動監視する, 観察する

□ **monoxide** 名一酸化物

□ **moonquake** 名月震《月に起こる地震のこと》

□ **morality** 名道徳, 徳性, 品行

□ **moreover** 副その上, さらに

□ **morning star** 明けの明星

□ **mostly** 副主として, 多くは, ほとんど

□ **motion** 名①運動, 移動 ②身振り, 動作

□ **move around** 動き回る, あちこち移動する, ～をあちこち動かす

□ **move away from** ～から遠ざかる

□ **movement** 名動き, 運動

□ **multi-planetary** 形多惑星の

□ **multiple** 形複合的な, 多様な

□ **multistage rocket** 多段(式)ロケット

□ **muscle** 名筋肉, 腕力

□ **mysterious** 形神秘的な, 謎めいた

□ **mystery** 名神秘, 不可思議

N

□ **naked** 形裸の, むき出しの **naked eye** 肉眼

□ **name after** ～にちなんで名付ける

□ **nanometer** 名ナノメートル《1メートルの10億分の1(10の-9乗メートル) の長さの単位》

□ **narrow** 動狭くなる［する］

□ **NASA** 略アメリカ航空宇宙局 (National Aeronautics and Space Administration)《アメリカ合衆国政府内における宇宙開発に関わる計画を担当する連邦機関》

□ **nation** 名国, 国家

□ **national** 形国家の, 全国の

□ **natural phenomena** 自然現象

□ **navigate** 動航行する, 飛行する

□ **navigation** 名航行, 航海, 操縦

□ **navigation satellite** 航行衛星

□ **Nazis** 名ナチス《ドイツの政党, 国家社会主義ドイツ労働者党の略称。また, その党員。Nazi の複数形》

□ **near-Earth asteroid** 地球近傍小惑星《地球の軌道を横切るような軌道を持つ小惑星》

□ **near-infrared light** 近赤外光《波長が約0.7～2.5μmの電磁波で, 赤色の可視光線に近い波長を持つ。可視光線と電波の中間に位置する波長を持つ光》

□ **nearly** 副①近くに, 親しく ②ほとんど, あやうく

□ **nebula** 名星雲

□ **nebulae** 名nebula (星雲) の複数形

□ **necessary** 形必要な, 必然の

□ **neighborhood** 名近所(の人々),

A
B
C
D
E
F
G
H
I
J
K
L
M
N
O
P
Q
R
S
T
U
V
W
X
Y
Z

付近

- [ ] **neighboring** 形 隣の, 近所の
- [ ] **Neil Armstrong** ニール・アームストロング《アメリカ合衆国の宇宙飛行士。人類で初めて月面に降り立った。1930-2012 年》
- [ ] **neither** 副《否定文に続いて》〜も…しない neither 〜 nor … 〜も…もない
- [ ] **Neptune** 名 海王星
- [ ] **network** 名 回路, 網状組織, ネットワーク
- [ ] **Neuralink** 名 ニューラリンク《脳に埋め込まれたブレイン・マシン・インタフェースを開発する会社で, イーロン・マスクらが共同設立した》
- [ ] **neutron star** 中性子星《大質量星が超新星爆発を起こした後に残る, ほぼ中性子だけで構成された超高密度の天体》
- [ ] **New Horizons** ニュー・ホライズンズ《アメリカ航空宇宙局（NASA）が 2006 年に打ち上げた, 人類初の冥王星を含む太陽系外縁天体の探査を行うための無人探査機》
- [ ] **New Zealand** ニュージーランド
- [ ] **newly** 副 再び, 最近, 新たに
- [ ] **nickel** 名 ニッケル, 白銅
- [ ] **nineteenth** 名《通例 the –》第 19 番目（の人［物］）, 19 日 形《通例 the –》第 19 番目の
- [ ] **nitrogen** 名 窒素
- [ ] **no longer** もはや〜でない［〜しない］
- [ ] **no matter** 〜を問わず, どうでもいい
- [ ] **no one** 誰も［一人も］〜ない
- [ ] **non-optical** 形 非光学式
- [ ] **non-optical telescope** 非光学式望遠鏡《可視光以外の電磁波や粒子を観測する装置。例えば, 赤外線望遠鏡, 電波望遠鏡, X 線望遠鏡, ガンマ線望遠鏡など》

- [ ] **non-visible light** 不可視光線
- [ ] **nor** 接 〜もまたない neither 〜 nor … 〜も…もない
- [ ] **North Korea** 北朝鮮《朝鮮民主主義人民共和国》
- [ ] **not 〜 but ...** 〜ではなくて…
- [ ] **not only 〜 but also ...** 〜だけでなく 〜もまた
- [ ] **nothing but** ただ〜だけ, 〜にすぎない, 〜のほかは何も…ない
- [ ] **notice** 気づく, 認める
- [ ] **now** 熟 from now 今から, これから
- [ ] **nuclear** 形 核の, 原子力の
- [ ] **nuclear arms race** 核軍備競争
- [ ] **nuclear bomb** 核爆弾
- [ ] **nuclear explosion** 核爆発
- [ ] **nuclear fusion** 核融合《軽い核種同士が融合してより重い核種になる核反応。非常に大きなエネルギーが発生する》
- [ ] **nuclear test** 核実験
- [ ] **nuclear weapon** 核兵器
- [ ] **nuclear-powered** 形 原子力を利用した
- [ ] **nursery** 名 ①育児室, 託児所 ②苗床, 養成所

O

- [ ] **object** 名 ①物, 事物 ②目的物, 対象
- [ ] **observation** 名 観察（力）, 注目
- [ ] **observe** 動 観察［観測］する, 監視［注視］する
- [ ] **observer** 名 観察者, オブザーバー
- [ ] **obstacle** 名 障害（物）, じゃま（な物）
- [ ] **occasionally** 副 時折, 時たま
- [ ] **occupy** 動 ①占領する, 保有する

②居住する ③占める ④（職に）つく，
従事する

□ **of** 熟 age of ～の時代 because of
～のために，～の理由で dream of
～を夢見る hundreds of 何百もの
～ instead of ～の代わりに，～を
しないで one of ～の1つ［人］ out
of ①～から外へ，～から抜け出して
②～から作り出して，～を材料とし
て speaking of ～について言えば
think of ～のことを考える，～を思
いつく，考え出す thousands of 何
千という world of ～の世界

□ **off** 熟 give off 発散する，放つ set
off 出発する，発射する take off 離
陸する

□ **offensive** 形 攻撃的な

□ **offer** 動 提供する

□ **Olympus Mons** オリンポス山
《火星最大の楯状火山。Mons（惑星表
面の山岳地形）としては，太陽系で最
大。標高は約25,000m》

□ **on** 熟 carry on ～を続ける depend on
～をあてにする，～しだいである on
board（乗り物などに）乗って，搭乗
して on the ground 地面に on the
other hand 一方，他方では on the
surface 外面は，うわべは pull on
～を引っ張る put ～ on ～を…の場
所に持ってくる walk on 歩き続ける
work on ～で働く，～に取り組む

□ **one** 熟 each one 各自 no one 誰
も［一人も］～ない one another お
互い one day（未来の）いつか one
of ～の1つ［人］

□ **one-sixth** 名 6分の1

□ **online** 副 オンラインで

□ **only** 熟 not only ～ but also … ～
だけでなく…もまた

□ **onto** 前 ～の上へ［に］

□ **open up** 広がる，広げる，開く，開
ける

□ **operate** 動（機械などが）動く，運
転する，管理する，操業する

□ **Operation Argus** アーガス作戦

《1958年にアメリカ国防脅威削減局
により南大西洋で実施された核兵器
とミサイルに関する秘密実験》

□ **operational** 形 使用できる，運転
可能な

□ **opportunity** 名 好機，適当な時期
［状況］

□ **Opportunity** 名 オポチュニティ
《は，アメリカ航空宇宙局（NASA）の
火星探査車で，マーズ・エクスプロ
レーション・ローバー計画で使用され
た2台の探査車のうちの2号機》

□ **opposite** 形 反対の，向こう側の

□ **optical** 形 眼の，光学（上）の

□ **optical telescope** 光学望遠鏡

□ **or so** ～かそこらで

□ **orbit** 名 ①軌道 ②活動［勢力］範囲
動 軌道に乗る［乗せる］

□ **orbital debris** 軌道上デブリ

□ **orbital rocket booster** 軌道
ロケットブースター《多段式の打ち上
げロケットの最初の段階，または長時
間燃焼する持続ロケットと並行して
使用される短時間燃焼するロケット》

□ **Orbital Sciences Corporation**
オービタル・サイエンシズ《かつて存
在したアメリカ合衆国の企業である。
人工衛星の製造・打ち上げを行って
おり，また打ち上げシステムグループ
はミサイル防衛とも関わっていた》

□ **ordinary** 形 普通の，通常の

□ **organic** 形 有機の organic
molecule 有機分子

□ **organism** 名 有機体，生物

□ **origin** 名 起源，出自

□ **originally** 副 元は，元来

□ **originate** 動 始まる，始める，起こ
す，生じる

□ **Orion** 名 オリオン《アメリカ航空宇
宙局（NASA）がスペースシャトルの
代替として開発中の有人ミッション
用の宇宙船》

□ **Orion** 名 オリオン座《オリオンはギ

リシア神話に登場する巨人の狩人》

- ☐ **Orion Arm** オリオン腕《銀河系の比較的小規模な渦状腕の1つであり, 現時点で太陽系が通過中の渦状腕》
- ☐ **other** 熟 each other お互いに on the other hand 一方, 他方では than any other ほかのどの〜よりも
- ☐ **otherwise** 副 さもないと, そうでなければ
- ☐ **out** 熟 find out 見つけ出す, 気がつく make 〜 out of … 〜を…から作る out of ①〜から外へ, 〜から抜け出して ②〜から作り出して, 〜を材料として run out of 〜を使い果たす set out 出発する spread out 広げる, 展開する stand out 突き出る, 目立つ step out of 〜から出る throw out 放り出す turn out to be 〜という結果になる
- ☐ **outer** 形 外の, 外側の
- ☐ **outer space** 宇宙 (空間)
- ☐ **Outer Space Treaty** 宇宙条約《国際的な宇宙法の基礎となった条約。宇宙空間における探査と利用の自由, 領有の禁止, 宇宙平和利用の原則, 国家への責任集中原則などが定められている》
- ☐ **outward** 副 外側へ
- ☐ **oval** 形 卵形の, 楕円形の
- ☐ **oval-shaped** 形 卵型の
- ☐ **oven** 名 かまど, 天火, オーブン
- ☐ **over** 熟 all over 〜中で, 全体に亘って, 〜の至る所で over time 時間とともに, そのうち
- ☐ **overcame** 動 overcome (勝つ) の過去
- ☐ **overcome** 動 勝つ, 打ち勝つ, 克服する
- ☐ **overpopulation** 名 人口過剰
- ☐ **oxygen** 名 酸素

P

- ☐ **Pacific Ocean** 太平洋
- ☐ **pack** 動 詰め込む
- ☐ **panel** 名 パネル
- ☐ **parade** 名 パレード, 行列
- ☐ **participate** 動 参加する, 加わる
- ☐ **particle** 名 粒子, 小さな粒, 微量
- ☐ **particularly** 副 特に, とりわけ
- ☐ **pass through** 〜を通る, 通行する
- ☐ **passage** 名 通過, 通行, 経過
- ☐ **passion** 名 情熱, (〜への) 熱中, 激怒
- ☐ **past** 形 過去の, この前の 名 過去 (の出来事)
- ☐ **patch** 名 1区画 patch of sky 空の一角
- ☐ **path** 名 進路, 通路
- ☐ **Pathfinder** 名 (マーズ・) パスファインダー《アメリカ航空宇宙局 (NASA) JPL (ジェット推進研究所) がディスカバリー計画の一環として行った火星探査計画, またはその探査機群の総称。1996年12月4日に地球を発ち, 1997年7月4日に火星に着陸》
- ☐ **pattern** 名 (思考や行動などの) パターン, 様式
- ☐ **pave** 動 舗装する pave the way for 〜の地固めをする, 〜の下地をつくる
- ☐ **payload** 名 ペイロード《(宇宙船に搭載される) 観測機器, 実験装置》
- ☐ **Paypal** 名 ペイパル《電子メールアカウントとインターネットを利用した決済サービスを提供するアメリカの企業》
- ☐ **peace** 熟 in peace 平和のうちに, 安心して
- ☐ **peaceful** 形 平和な, 穏やかな
- ☐ **peak** 名 頂点, 最高点
- ☐ **penguin** 名 ペンギン

Word List

□ **per** 前 ～につき，～ごとに

□ **performance** 名 ①実行，行為 ②成績，できばえ，業績

□ **perhaps** 副 たぶん，ことによると

□ **period** 名 期，期間，時代

□ **permanent** 形 永続する，永久の，長持ちする **permanent presence** 恒久的駐留

□ **perseverance** 名 忍耐(力)，根気

□ **Perseverance** 名 パーサヴィアランス《NASAのマーズ2020ミッションの一環として，火星のジェゼロクレーターを探査するためのマーズ・ローバー。19台のカメラと2つのマイクを搭載する他，小型ヘリコプター「インジェニュイティ」を搭載している》

□ **perspective** 名 観点

□ **phenomenon** 名 現象，事象

□ **Phobetor** 名 ポベートール《PSR B1257+12が伴ってる太陽系外惑星の一つ。パルサーから約0.36天文単位の距離を約66日間かけて公転，質量は地球の4倍以上》

□ **Phobos** 名 フォボス《火星の二つの衛星の一つ》

□ **phospine** 名 ホスフィン，水酸化リン

□ **photo** 名 写真

□ **photosynthesize** 動 光合成する

□ **physical** 形 身体の，肉体の

□ **physicist** 名 物理学者

□ **physics** 名 物理学

□ **picture** 熟 **take a picture** 写真を撮る

□ **Pillars of Creation (POC)** 創造の柱《1995年ハッブル宇宙望遠鏡が撮影した，わし星雲の中にある星間物質が集まった3本の柱。柱の先端には，卵と呼ばれるたくさんの小さな突起があり，そこで星が作られていることが確認された》

□ **pinwheel** 名 風車，回転花火

□ **pioneer** 名 開拓者，先駆者

□ **place** 熟 **take place** 行われる，起こる

□ **placement** 名 置くこと，配置

□ **plague** 動 ～で悩ます

□ **plain** 名 高原

□ **planet-building site** 惑星形成の場所

□ **planetesimal** 名 微惑星《太陽系の形成初期に存在したと考えられている微小天体》

□ **planet-making** 名 惑星形成

□ **plaque** 名 額，飾り板

□ **platform** 名 プラットホーム，壇

□ **platinum** 名 白金，プラチナ

□ **player** 名 競技者，選手

□ **Pluto** 名 冥王星

□ **polar** 形 極(地)の

□ **pole** 名 極(地)

□ **polish** 動 磨く，磨きをかける

□ **political** 形 政治の

□ **politics** 名 政治(学)，政策

□ **pollution** 名 汚染，公害

□ **Poltergeist** 名 ポルターガイスト《PSR B1257+12が伴ってる太陽系外惑星の一つ。パルサーから約0.46天文単位の距離を約98日間かけて公転，地球の4倍近い質量》

□ **popular among** 《be –》～の間で人気がある

□ **pose** 動 引き起こす

□ **position** 名 位置，場所

□ **possess** 動 持つ，所有する

□ **possibility** 名 可能性，見込み，将来性

□ **possible** 形 ①可能な ②ありうる，起こりうる **make it possible for ～ to …** ～が…できるようにする

□ **possibly** 副 あるいは，たぶん

A B C D E F G H I J K L M N O **P** Q R S T U V W X Y Z

- □ **potential** 形 可能性がある, 潜在的な 名 可能性, 潜在能力
- □ **powerful** 形 力強い, 実力のある, 影響力のある
- □ **predict** 予測［予想］する
- □ **pre-launch** 形 発射準備(中)の
- □ **prepared** 形 準備［用意］のできた prepared for 〜に備える
- □ **presence** 名 存在すること permanent presence 恒久的駐留
- □ **preserve** 動 保存［保護］する, 保つ
- □ **President** 名 大統領
- □ **pressure** 名 プレッシャー, 圧力
- □ **prevent** 動 妨げる, じゃまする
- □ **previous** 形 前の, 先の
- □ **previously** 副 あらかじめ, 以前に［は］
- □ **price** 名 値段, 代価 come at a price 高くつく, 相当の犠牲となる
- □ **pride** 名 誇り, 自慢, 自尊心
- □ **primitive** 形 原始的, 初期の, 旧式の
- □ **principle** 名 原理, 原則
- □ **private** 形 民間の, 私立の
- □ **probably** 副 たぶん, あるいは
- □ **probe** 名 宇宙探査用装置
- □ **process** 名 過程, 経過, 進行
- □ **product** 名 ①製品, 産物 ②成果, 結果
- □ **prohibit** 動 禁止する
- □ **project** 名 計画, プロジェクト
- □ **proportion** 名 割合, 比率
- □ **propose** 動 提案する
- □ **protective** 形 保護する, 保護(用)の protective suit 保護［防護］服
- □ **protector** 名 保護者
- □ **proven** 形 証明された
- □ **provide** 動 供給する, 用意する

- □ **provider** 名 プロバイダー, インターネット接続業者
- □ **Proxima Centauri** プロキシマ・ケンタウリ《ケンタウルス座の方向に4.246光年離れた位置にある赤色矮星。太陽系に最も近い恒星として知られている》
- □ **PSR B1257+12** PSR B1257+12《太陽から約980光年の距離にあるパルサー(高速で自転する中性子星の一種。パルス状の可視光線, 電波, X線を発生する天体)。2007年までに3つの太陽系外惑星が見つかっている》
- □ **public** 形 公の
- □ **pull on** 〜を引っ張る
- □ **pursue** 動 ①追う, つきまとう ②追求する, 従事する
- □ **put 〜 on** 〜を…の場所に持ってくる
- □ **puzzle** 名 ①難問, 当惑 ②パズル

Q

- □ **quasar** 名 恒星状天体, 準星, クエーサー《非常に離れた距離に存在し極めて明るく輝いているために, 光学望遠鏡では内部構造が見えず, 恒星のような点光源に見える天体のこと》
- □ **quest** 名 追求, 探求, 冒険の旅
- □ **quickly** 副 敏速に, 急いで
- □ **quite a few** かなり多くの

R

- □ **radiating** 形 放射する, 照射する, 放散する
- □ **radiation** 名 放射(能), 放射線
- □ **radio satellite** 衛星ラジオ
- □ **radio telescope** 電波望遠鏡《電波を収束させて天体を観測する装置の総称》

Word List

□ **radio wave** 電波

□ **radioactive** 形放射能の, 放射性の

□ **raise** 動①上げる, 高める ②起こす

□ **random** 形手当たり次第の, 無作為の

□ **randomly** 副無作為に, 不規則に

□ **range** 動およぶ

□ **rapidly** 副速く, 急速, すばやく, 迅速に

□ **rate** 名割合, 率

□ **rather** 副①むしろ, かえって ②かなり, いくぶん, やや ③それどころか逆に **rather than** ～よりむしろ

□ **ray** 名光線, 放射線

□ **react** 動反応する, 対処する

□ **reaction** 名反応, 反動, 反抗, 影響

□ **reality** 名現実, 実在, 真実(性)

□ **realize** 動理解する, 実現する

□ **recently** 副近ごろ, 最近

□ **record** 名記録, 登録, 履歴 動①記録[登録]する ②録音[録画]する

□ **recover** 動取り戻す

□ **recruit** 動(人材を)募集する

□ **recycle** 動再生利用する, 再循環させる

□ **red giant** 赤色巨星《恒星が主系列星を終えたあとの進化段階である。大気が膨張し, その大きさは地球の公転軌道半径から火星のそれに相当する。肉眼で観察すると赤く見えることから, 「赤色」巨星と呼ばれる》

□ **Red Planet** 赤い惑星《火星の俗称》

□ **reddish** 形赤みがかかった

□ **reduce** 動減じる

□ **re-entry** 名(宇宙船などの大気圏への) 再突入

□ **refer to** ～に言及する, ～と呼ぶ

□ **reflect** 動映る, 反響する, 反射する

□ **reflecting telescope** 反射望遠鏡《鏡を組み合わせた望遠鏡》

□ **refracting telescope** 屈折望遠鏡《レンズを組み合わせた望遠鏡》

□ **region** 名地域, 範囲

□ **regular** 形①規則的な ②定期的な, 一定の, 習慣的

□ **regulate** 動規制[統制, 調節]する

□ **regulation** 名規則, 規定, 規制

□ **rejoin** 動復帰する, 再び一緒になる

□ **release** 動解き放す

□ **remain** 動①残っている, 残る ②(～の)ままである[いる]

□ **remarkable** 形⑴異常な, 例外的な ②注目に値する, すばらしい

□ **reminder** 名思い出させるもの

□ **remnant** 名(～の)残り, なごり

□ **remote** 形(距離・時間的に)遠い, 遠隔の

□ **removal** 名除去, 移動

□ **remove** 動取り去る, 除去する

□ **reorganize** 動再編成する, 再組織する

□ **repair** 動修理[修繕]する 名修理, 修繕

□ **require** 動必要とする, 要する

□ **research** 名調査, 研究

□ **reshape** 動形を整える[作り直す]

□ **resource** 名資源

□ **response** 名応答, 反応, 返答

□ **responsible** 形責任のある, 信頼できる, 確実な

□ **result** 名結果, 成り行き, 成績 **as a result of** ～の結果(として) 動(結果として)起こる, 生じる, 結局～になる

□ **retrograde** 形(惑星や衛星が)逆行の《地球を回る月や, 太陽を回る地球の回転方向と逆の方向を指す》

□ **return to** ～に戻る, ～に帰る

□ **reusable** 形 再利用［再使用］できる

□ **reuse** 動 再利用する

□ **reveal** 動 明らかにする，暴露する，もらす

□ **revolutionize** 動 大変革［革命］をもたらす，根本的に変える

□ **revolve** 動 回転する［させる］，中心に回る

□ **Richard Nixon** リチャード・ニクソン《アメリカ合衆国の政治家。同国第37代大統領。在任1969–1974年》

□ **ring** 名 輪，円形

□ **rise** 熟 give rise to ～を生じさせる

□ **risk** 名 危険

□ **risky** 形 危険な，冒険的な，リスクの伴う

□ **rivalry** 名 競争，ライバル，敵対

□ **Robert Goddard** ロバート・ゴダード《アメリカの発明家・ロケット研究者。「ロケットの父」と呼ばれる。1882–1945年》

□ **Robert Hooke** ロバート・フック《イギリスの自然哲学者，建築家，博物学者，生物学者。1635–1703年》

□ **robot** 名 ロボット

□ **robotic** 形 ロボットの［のような・による］

□ **robotic arm** ロボットアーム

□ **robotic spacecraft** 無人宇宙船，宇宙ロボット《宇宙空間や宇宙ステーションの内外，惑星の表面において活動するロボット》

□ **rocket** 名 ロケット

□ **rocket equation** ロケット方程式，ツィオルコフスキーの公式《1897年にコンスタンチン・ツィオルコフスキーによって示されたロケット推進に関する公式》

□ **rocket stage** ロケットのステージ［段階］

□ **rocky** 形 岩の多い

□ **role** 名 役割，任務

□ **Roman** 形 ローマ（人）の 名 ①ローマ人［市民］ ②（ローマ）カトリック教

□ **rotate** 動 回転する

□ **rotation** 名 回転，自転

□ **rotten** 形 腐った

□ **rough** 形 荒々しい

□ **rover** 名 惑星探査機，ローバー

□ **rugged** 形 ごつごつした

□ **run out of** ～を使い果たす

□ **Russia** 名 ロシア《国名》

□ **Russian** 形 ロシア（人・語）の 名 ①ロシア人 ②ロシア語

□ **rust-colored** 形 さび色の

S

□ **sadly** 副 悲しそうに，不幸にも

□ **safely** 副 安全に，間違いなく

□ **safety** 名 安全，無事，確実

□ **Sagittarius a*** いて座A*《天の川銀河の中心にある明るくコンパクトな天文電波源。より大規模な構造の電波源領域であるいて座Aの一部》

□ **Sagittarius Dwarf Irregular Galaxy** いて座矮小不規則銀河《局所銀河群（太陽系の所属する天の川銀河が所属する銀河群）に属する矮小銀河である。地球から約400万光年の距離にある》

□ **sail** 名 帆

□ **sailing ship** 帆船

□ **same ～ as …** 《the –》…と同じ（ような）～

□ **sample** 名 標本

□ **sand** 名 砂

□ **satellite** 名 （人工）衛星

□ **Saturn** 名 土星

□ **Saturn V** サターンV《1967年から

Word List

1973 年にかけてアメリカ合衆国のアポロ計画およびスカイラブ計画で使用された, 使い捨て方式の液体燃料多段式ロケット》

□ **save money** コストを削減する, 貯金する

□ **scar** 图傷跡

□ **scarcity** 图欠乏, 不足

□ **scatter** 動①ばらまく, 分散する ②《be -ed》散在する

□ **scattered** 形散らばった

□ **science fiction** サイエンス・フィクション, 空想科学小説

□ **scientific** 形科学の, 科学的な

□ **scoop** 图スコップ, 小型シャベル

□ **scorching-hot** 形焼け付くように暑い, やけどするほど熱い

□ **Sea of Tranquility** 静かの海《月の表面にある月の海の一つ。アポロ 11 号の月着陸船が着陸した場所》

□ **search** 動捜し求める, 調べる

□ **secret** 图秘密

□ **security** 图安全保障

□ **see ~ as …** ~を…と見る

□ **seek** 動捜し求める, 求める

□ **seem** 動 (~に) 見える, (~のように) 思われる

□ **seen as** 《be – 》~として見られる

□ **sense** 图①感覚, 感じ ②《-s》意識, 正気, 本性 ③常識, 分別, センス ④意味

□ **sensor** 图センサー, 感知装置

□ **separate** 動分ける, 分かれる

□ **serious** 形重大な, 深刻な

□ **serve** 動 (役目を) 果たす, 務める, 役に立つ

□ **service module** サービスモジュール《有人宇宙カプセルに付随する無人の宇宙船で, 電気システムや推進システムなどの重要なサブシステムを搭載している》

□ **set off** 出発する, 発射する

□ **set out** 出発する

□ **setback** 图後退

□ **seventeenth** 图 17, 17 人 [個] 形 17 の, 17 人 [個] の

□ **severe** 形厳しい, 深刻な, 激しい

□ **shadow** 图影

□ **shake** 動振る, 揺れる, 揺さぶる, 震える

□ **shape** 图形, 姿, 型 動形づくる

□ **shaped** 形~の形をした

□ **shield** 動保護する, 遮蔽する

□ **shift** 動移す, 変える, 転嫁する

□ **shine** 動光る, 輝く

□ **shore** 图岸, 海岸, 陸

□ **short** 熟for short 略して

□ **showcase** 動見せる, 展示する

□ **shown** 動show (見せる) の過去分詞

□ **shrink** 動縮む, 縮小する

□ **shrouded** 形~に覆われた, ~に覆い隠された

□ **Siberia** 图シベリア

□ **sibling** 图きょうだい《誕生の順・性別を問わない》

□ **side** 图側, 横, そば

□ **sideways** 副横 (向き) に, 斜めに

□ **Sierra Nevada Corporation** シエラ・ネヴァダ・コーポレーション《アメリカ合衆国ネバダ州にある航空機・宇宙船の開発製造会社》

□ **signal** 图信号, 合図

□ **significant** 形①重要な, 有意義な ②大幅な, 著しい

□ **similar** 形同じような, 類似した, 相似の be similar to ~に似ている

□ **since** 熟ever since それ以来ずっと

□ **single** 形たった 1 つの

□ **singularity** 图特異点《宇宙が膨

A B C D E F G H I J K L M N O P Q R **S** T U V W X Y Z

163

らむ前に存在した無限に小さな点》

- **sky-gazer** 名 天体観測者
- **slightly** 副 わずかに, いささか
- **slowly** 副 遅く, ゆっくり
- **smooth** 形 静かな, 平穏な
- **so** 熟 and so そこで, それだから, それで or so 〜かそこらで so far 今までのところ, これまでは so that 〜するために, それで, 〜できるように so 〜 that … 非常に〜なので…
- **soccer field** サッカー場
- **social media** ソーシャルメディア
- **society** 名 社会, 世間
- **soil** 名 土, 土地
- **Sojourner** 名 ソジャーナ《パスファインダーに搭載されたマーズ・ローバー（探査車）の名前》
- **solar** 形 太陽の, 太陽光線を利用した
- **solar arrays** ソーラーアレイ《太陽光発電装置》
- **solar flare** 太陽フレア《太陽の表面に起きる爆発》
- **solar system** 太陽系
- **solar wind** 太陽風《太陽から吹き出す極めて高温で電離した粒子（プラズマ）のこと》
- **solid** 形 ①固体[固形]の ②頑丈な
- **solidify** 動 凝固する[させる], 固体化する
- **solo** 形 単独の
- **solution** 名 解決, 解明, 回答
- **solve** 動 解く, 解決する
- **someday** 副 いつか, そのうち
- **somehow** 副 ①どうにかこうにか, ともかく, 何とかして ②どういうわけか
- **something** 代 ①ある物, 何か ②いくぶん, 多少
- **sometimes** 副 時々, 時たま

- **somewhere** 副 ①どこかへ[に] ②いつか, およそ
- **sound like** 〜のように聞こえる
- **southern** 形 南の, 南向きの, 南からの
- **Soviet** 形 ソ連の
- **Soviet Union** ソビエト社会主義共和国連邦, ソ連（Union of Soviet Socialist Republics）《1917-1991年》
- **space age** 宇宙時代
- **space agency** 宇宙機関
- **space debris** スペースデブリ, 宇宙ゴミ《地球を周回する人工衛星・打ち上げロケットの残骸》
- **space domain** 宇宙領域
- **space exploration** 宇宙探検[探査]
- **Space Force** 宇宙軍
- **space junk** 宇宙ゴミ《地球を周回する人工衛星・打ち上げロケットの残骸》
- **Space Launch System (SLS)** スペース・ローンチ・システム《アメリカ航空宇宙局（NASA）により開発・運用されている, スペースシャトルから派生した大型打ち上げロケット》
- **space probe** 宇宙探査機
- **space race** 宇宙開発競争《冷戦中にアメリカ合衆国とソビエト連邦との間で宇宙開発をめぐって戦われた, 非公式の競争》
- **space shuttle** スペースシャトル《かつてアメリカ航空宇宙局（NASA）が1981年から2011年にかけて135回打ち上げた再使用をコンセプトに含んだ有人宇宙船》
- **space station** 宇宙ステーション
- **space technology** 宇宙技術
- **space-based telescope** 宇宙望遠鏡
- **spacecraft** 名 宇宙船
- **spaceship** 名 宇宙船

- **SpaceX** 名 スペースX《カリフォルニア州ホーソーンに本社を置くアメリカの航空宇宙メーカーであり、宇宙輸送サービス会社である他、衛星インターネットアクセスプロバイダでもある。2002年にイーロン・マスクによって設立》

- **sparkling** 形 輝く、きらめく

- **speaking of** ～について言えば

- **specialized** 形 専門の、分化した

- **species** 名 種、種類、人種

- **specific** 形 明確な、はっきりした、具体的な

- **spectacle** 名 光景

- **spectrometer** 名 分光器《光の電磁波スペクトルを測定する光学機器全般を指す》

- **speculate** 動 思索する、推測する

- **speed** 名 速力、速度

- **sphere** 名 球体、天体

- **spin** 動 ぐるぐる回る、スピンする 名 回転

- **spinning** 形 (軸の周りを)回転する

- **spiral** 形 らせん状の、渦巻き型の

- **spiral galaxy** 渦巻銀河《恒星が密集した丸い中心核から渦巻状の腕が出て(腕の先がさらに枝分れするものも多い)いる銀河》

- **Spirit** 名 スピリット《アメリカ航空宇宙局(NASA)の火星探査車。マーズ・エクスプロレーション・ローバー計画でオポチュニティと共に火星に送られた無人探査車の一つ》

- **split** 動 裂く、裂ける、割る、割れる、分裂させる[する]

- **spot** 動 ～を見つける

- **spread out** 広げる、展開する

- **Sputnik** 名 スプートニク1号のこと

- **Sputnik 1** スプートニク1号《ソビエト連邦が1957年10月4日に打ち上げた世界初の人工衛星》

- **square kilometer** 平方キロ

- **stabilize** 動 安定させる、固定する

- **stage** 名 段階

- **stakeholder** 名 利害関係者

- **stand out** 突き出る、目立つ

- **star cluster** 星団《同じガスから誕生した、互いの重力相互作用によって結びついた恒星の集団》

- **StarChips** 名 スターチップ《ブレークスルー・スターショット計画で使用される、1辺が1メートルほどの極薄の帆を取り付けた切手サイズの超小型宇宙船》

- **Starfish Prime** スターフィッシュ・プライム《米国が実施した高高度核実験。1962年7月9日にジョンストン環礁から打ち上げられ、宇宙で実施された最大の核実験》

- **Starlink** 名 スターリンク《アメリカ合衆国の民間企業スペースXが運用している衛星インターネットアクセスサービス、並びにこれを実現する衛星コンステレーション(多数個の人工衛星の一群・システム)》

- **starry** 形 星の(多い)、星明かりの

- **Starship** 名 スターシップ《アメリカの企業スペースX社が開発中の完全再使用型の二段式超大型ロケットかつ宇宙船》

- **stationary** 形 静止した

- **step out of** ～から出る

- **stepping stone** 踏み石、足がかり

- **stick** 動 くっつく、くっつける

- **stickiness** 名 粘着性

- **stopover point** 中継地

- **storm** 名 嵐、暴風雨

- **strategic** 形 戦略的な、戦略上の

- **strategy** 名 戦略、作戦、方針

- **stream** 名 小川、流れ

- **stress** 名 ストレス

- **stretch** 動 引き伸ばす、広がる、広

げる

- □ **striking** 形著しい, 目立つ
- □ **strip** 動裸にする, はぐ, 取り去る
- □ **structure** 名構造, 骨組み, 仕組み
- □ **struggle** 動もがく, 奮闘する
- □ **stuck** 動 stick（刺さる）の過去, 過去分詞 **get stuck in** 〜にはまり込む
- □ **stuff** 名材料, 原料
- □ **suburb** 名周辺地区
- □ **such as** たとえば〜, 〜のような
- □ **such 〜 that ...** 非常に〜なので ...
- □ **suck** 動吸い込む
- □ **suffocating** 形息の詰まるような
- □ **suggest** 動①提案する ②示唆する
- □ **suit** 名スーツ **protective suit** 保護［防護］服
- □ **sunlight** 名日光
- □ **sunrise** 名日の出
- □ **sunset** 名日没, 夕焼け
- □ **super** 形超一流の, 特大の
- □ **super Earth** スーパーアース《巨大地球型惑星。太陽系外惑星のうち地球の数倍程度の質量を持ち, かつ主成分が岩石や金属などの固体成分と推定された惑星のこと》
- □ **Super Heavy** スーパーヘビー《スターシップの1段目のブースター部分》
- □ **supermassive** 形超大質量の
- □ **supernova** 名超新星《大質量の恒星や近接連星系の白色矮星が起こす大規模な爆発（超新星爆発）によって輝く天体のこと》
- □ **supernovae** 名 supernova（超新星）の複数
- □ **support** 動支える, 支持する
- □ **sure** 熟 **for sure** 確かに **make sure** 確かめる, 確認する
- □ **surface** 名①表面, 水面 ②うわべ,

外見 **on the surface** 外面は, うわべは

- □ **surround** 動囲む, 包囲する
- □ **surrounding** 名《-s》周囲の状況, 環境
- □ **surveillance** 名監視, 監督, 見張り
- □ **survival** 名生き残ること
- □ **survive** 動生き残る, 存続する
- □ **sustainability** 名持続可能性
- □ **sustainable** 形支えられる, 持続できる
- □ **swan** 名ハクチョウ（白鳥）
- □ **swift** 形速い, 迅速な
- □ **swing** 名揺れ, 振ること, 振動
- □ **swirl around** 渦巻く
- □ **swirling** 形グルグル回る, 渦巻く
- □ **symbol** 名シンボル, 象徴

T

- □ **tail** 名尾, しっぽ
- □ **take a picture** 写真を撮る
- □ **take off** 離陸する
- □ **take place** 行われる, 起こる
- □ **take 〜 to ...** 〜を…に連れて行く
- □ **tale** 名話, 物語
- □ **tapestry** 名タペストリー, つづれ織り
- □ **target** 名標的, 目的物, 対象
- □ **taste** 動味がする
- □ **teaspoon** 名茶さじ, ティースプーン
- □ **technical** 形技術（上）の, 工業の, 専門の
- □ **technician** 名技術者, 専門家
- □ **technological** 名技術上の, (科学）技術の

166

□ **technology** 名 テクノロジー, 科学技術

□ **telescope** 名 望遠鏡

□ **television** 名 テレビ

□ **Telstar 1** テルスター1号《アメリカ航空宇宙局（NASA）が打ち上げた通信放送衛星。1962年（昭和37年）7月10日にケープカナベラル空軍基地から打ち上げられ, パリからアメリカへのテレビ中継に成功した》

□ **temperature** 名 温度, 体温

□ **tend** 動 （〜の）傾向がある, （〜）しがちである

□ **term** 名 語, 用語

□ **terrain** 名 地形, 地勢

□ **Tesla** 名 テスラ《テキサス州オースティンに本社を置く, アメリカの電動輸送機器およびクリーンエネルギー関連企業, 及び, 同社が製造販売する自動車のブランドや自動車自体の通称》

□ **testament** 名 証左, あかし

□ **than** 熟 rather than 〜よりむしろ than any other ほかのどの〜よりも

□ **thanks to** 〜のおかげで, 〜の結果

□ **that** 熟 after that その後 so that 〜するために それで 〜できるように so 〜 that … 非常に〜なので… such 〜 that … 非常に〜なので…

□ **theater** 名 劇場

□ **theme** 名 主題, テーマ

□ **therefore** 副 したがって, それゆえ, その結果

□ **thick** 形 厚い, 密集した, 濃厚な

□ **thin** 形 薄い

□ **think of** 〜のことを考える, 〜を思いつく, 考え出す

□ **thirst** 名 （のどの）渇き, （〜に対する）渇望, 切望

□ **thirteenth** 名 第13番目（の人［物］）, 13日 形 第13番目の

□ **this** 熟 at this time 現時点では, このとき in this way このようにして

□ **though** 接 ①にもかかわらず, 〜だが ②たとえ〜でも even though 〜であるけれども, 〜にもかかわらず 副 しかし

□ **thousands of** 何千という

□ **threat** 名 おどし, 脅迫

□ **thrive** 動 よく育つ, 繁栄する

□ **through** 熟 pass through 〜を通る, 通行する

□ **throughout** 前 ①〜中, 〜を通じて ②〜のいたるところに

□ **throw out** 放り出す

□ **thus** 副 ①このように ②これだけ ③かくて, だから

□ **Tianwen-1** 名 天問1号《中華人民共和国が2020年7月23日に打ち上げに成功した火星探査ミッションで用いる探査機の名称》

□ **tide** 名 潮, 潮流

□ **tilt** 名 傾斜

□ **time** 熟 as time passed 時がたつにつれて at a time 一度に at this time 現時点では, このとき in time 間に合って, やがて over time 時間とともに, そのうち the last time この前〜したとき times as … as A A の〜倍の…

□ **timeless** 形 永久の, 時間に左右されない

□ **tiny** 形 ちっぽけな, とても小さい

□ **Titan** 名 タイタン《土星の第6衛星で最大の衛星》

□ **ton** 名 ①トン《重量・容積単位》 ②《-s》たくさん

□ **tool** 名 道具, 用具, 工具

□ **total** 名 全体, 合計

□ **tour** 名 ツアー, 見て回ること, 視察

□ **towering** 形 そびえ立つ, 高くそびえる

□ **trace** 名 跡, こん跡

□ **tracking** 名（痕跡などを）たどること，追う［追跡する］こと

□ **traditional** 形 伝統的な

□ **traffic** 名 通行，往来，交通（量）
traffic jam 交通渋滞

□ **tragedy** 名 悲劇，惨劇

□ **tragic** 形 悲劇の，痛ましい

□ **Tranquility Base** 静かの基地
《1969年7月20日にアポロ11号の月着陸船が着陸した場所》

□ **transform** 動 ①変形［変化］する，変える ②変換する

□ **transmit** 動 ①送る ②伝える，伝わる

□ **transparent** 形 透明な，透けて見える

□ **trap** 名 わな 動 わなを仕掛ける，わなで捕らえる

□ **traveler** 名 旅行者

□ **traveling** 名 旅行

□ **treasure** 名 財宝，宝物

□ **treaty** 名 条約，協定

□ **tremendous** 形 すさまじい，とても大きい

□ **tricky** 形 油断のならない，扱いにくい，ずるい

□ **trigger** 名 引き金，きっかけ，要因

□ **trillion** 名 1兆

□ **Triton** 名 トリトン《海王星最大の衛星で，海王星で発見された初めての衛星》

□ **truss** 名 トラス《梁や桁などの部材を三角形に組み合わせて作る剛性の高い構造》

□ **truth** 名 ①真理，事実，本当 ②誠実，忠実さ

□ **Tsiolkovsky** 名 （コンスタンチン・）ツィオルコフスキー《ロシア帝国生まれのロケット研究者，物理学者。人工衛星や宇宙船の示唆，多段式ロケット，軌道エレベータなどの考案や，宇宙旅行の可能性としてロケ

ットで宇宙に行けることを証明した。1857-1935年》

□ **tube** 名 管，筒

□ **Tunguska** 名 ツングースカ《ロシアの地名。1908年6月30日7時2分（現地時間）頃，ロシア帝国領中央シベリア，エニセイ川支流のポドカメンナヤ・ツングースカ川上流（現・ロシア連邦クラスノヤルスク地方）ヴァナヴァラ北の上空で隕石による爆発が起こった》

□ **turn into** ～に変わる

□ **turn out to be** ～という結果になる

□ **TV signal** テレビジョン信号

□ **twin** 形 双子の，1対の

□ **twinkle** 動 きらきら光る，輝く

□ **twinkling** 形 キラキラ輝く

□ **typhoon** 名 台風

□ **typical** 形 典型的な，象徴的な

U

□ **ultimate** 形 最終の，究極の

□ **ultraviolet** 形 紫外線の

□ **ultraviolet light** 紫外線（光）

□ **unable** 形 《be - to ～》～することができない

□ **uncertain** 形 不確かな，確信がない

□ **uncontrollable** 形 制御できない

□ **uncover** 動 ふたを取る，覆いを取る

□ **underserved** 形 十分なサービスを受けていない

□ **understanding** 名 理解，意見の一致，了解

□ **underwater** 副 水面下で，水中で

□ **undiscovered** 形 発見されていない

□ **unexplored** 形 探検［踏査・調査］

されていない

□ **unfold** 動 展開する，～を開く［広げる］

□ **unfortunately** 副 不幸にも，運悪く

□ **unimaginably** 副 想像を絶するほど

□ **unique** 形 唯一の，ユニークな，独自の

□ **unite** 動 ①1つにする［なる］，合わせる，結ぶ ②結束する，団結する

□ **United States** (アメリカ) 合衆国

□ **universe** 名《the ~ /the U-》宇宙，全世界

□ **unknown** 形 知られていない，不明の

□ **unlike** 前 ～と違って

□ **unlock** 動 かぎを開ける，解く

□ **unmanned** 形 無人 (操縦) の

□ **unprecedented** 形 前例［先例］のない，異例の

□ **unpredictable** 形 予測できない，予測不可能な

□ **unravel** 動 (謎などを) 解く

□ **unreachable** 形 手の届かない

□ **unusual** 形 普通でない，珍しい，見［聞き］慣れない

□ **unveil** 動 (秘密などを) 明かす，明らかにする

□ **up** 熟 be made up of ～で構成されている blow up 破裂する［させる］ look up 見上げる made up of ～で作られた，～で構成［形成］された open up 広がる，広げる，開く，開ける up to ～まで，～に至るまで use up ～を使い果たす warm up 暖まる，温める

□ **upon** 前《場所・接触》～ (の上) に

□ **Uranus** 名 天王星

□ **urgency** 名 緊急性

□ **urgent** 形 緊急の，差し迫った

□ **Ursa Major** おおぐま座

□ **use up** ～を使い果たす

□ **used** 動 ①use (使う) の過去，過去分詞 ②《- to》よく～したものだ，以前は～であった 形 ①慣れている，《get［become］– to》～に慣れてくる ②使われた，中古の

□ **USSR** 略 ソビエト社会主義共和国連邦，ソ連 (Union of Soviet Socialist Republics)《1917-1991年》

□ **Utopia Planitia** ユートピア平原《火星の北半球の中緯度地方に存在する広大な盆地に付けられた名称》

V

□ **V-2** 名 V2ロケット《第二次世界大戦中にドイツが開発した世界初の軍事用液体燃料ロケットであり，弾道ロケット。後にアメリカ合衆国でアポロ計画を主導したヴェルナー・フォン・ブラウンが計画に参加し設計を行ったことで知られる》

□ **vacuum** 名 真空

□ **valley** 名 谷，谷間

□ **valuable** 形 貴重な，価値のある，役に立つ

□ **value** 名 価値，値打ち

□ **vapor** 名 蒸気，湯気 water vapor 水蒸気

□ **variety** 名 種類

□ **various** 形 変化に富んだ，さまざまの，たくさんの

□ **vast** 形 広大な，巨大な，ばく大な

□ **vastness** 名 広大さ

□ **vehicle** 名 乗り物，車，車両

□ **Venera** 名 ベネラ《ソビエト連邦の金星探査計画。他の惑星大気圏への探査機の投入，惑星表面への軟着陸，惑星表面からの映像転送，高解像度レーダーによる惑星表面の地図の作成などこの探査計画ではさまざまな人類初の試みが行われた》

□ **venture** 動思い切って～する，危険にさらす

□ **Venus** 名金星

□ **versatile** 形多方面の，多目的な，多芸多才の

□ **version** 名バージョン，版

□ **vessel** 名（大型の）船

□ **vibrant** 形響き渡る，活気のある，（色が）鮮やかな

□ **victory** 名勝利，優勝

□ **Viking 1** バイキング1号《NASAのバイキング計画で火星に送られた2機の探査機のうち最初の1機。1975年8月20日にで打ち上げられ，オービタは1976年6月19日に火星軌道に入り，オービタから分離したランダーは7月20日11:56:06 UTにクリュセ平原の西部に着陸した》

□ **Viking 2** バイキング2号《火星探査計画であるバイキング計画の一部で，バイキング1号に続くもの。1975年9月9日にケープカナベラル空軍基地より打ち上げられた。1976年8月7日にオービタは火星軌道に投入され，1976年9月3日にランダーがオービタから分離し，22:37:50 UTにユートピア平原に着陸した》

□ **violent** 形暴力的な，激しい

□ **Virgin Galactic** ヴァージン・ギャラクティック《ヴァージン・グループ会長のリチャード・ブランソンが設立した宇宙旅行ビジネスを行う会社》

□ **visible** 形目に見える，明らかな

□ **visible light** 可視光（線）

□ **vision** 名未来像，ビジョン

□ **visionary** 形先見の明のある，ビジョンを持った

□ **volcanic** 形火山の

□ **volcanic activity** 火山活動

□ **volcano** 名火山，噴火口

□ **von Braun** （ヴェルナー・）フォン・ブラウン《工学者であり，ロケット技術開発の最初期における最重要指導者のひとり。1912-1977年》

□ **voyage** 名航海，航行

□ **Voyager** 名ボイジャー《NASAの無人宇宙探査機。ボイジャー1号（1977年9月5日打ち上げ）と2号（1977年8月20日打ち上げ）の2機がある》

□ **Voyager 2** ボイジャー2号《NASA（アメリカ航空宇宙局）により1977年8月20日に打ち上げられた，木星よりも遠くの外惑星及び衛星の探査を目的として開発・運用されている無人宇宙探査機。木星（1979年）・土星（1981年）・天王星（1986年）・海王星（1989年）の「グランドツアー」を初めて実現した探査機となった》

W

□ **walk on** 歩き続ける

□ **war criminal** 戦争犯罪人，戦犯

□ **warm up** 暖まる，温める

□ **warn** 動警告する，用心させる

□ **warp** 動曲がる，そる，ゆがむ

□ **water vapor** 水蒸気

□ **wave** 名波，うねり

□ **wavelength** 名波長

□ **way** 熟 along the way 途中で，これまでに，この先 in this way このようにして way to ～する方法

□ **wealth** 名富

□ **weapon** 名武器，兵器

□ **weaponized** 形兵器化［武器化］された

□ **weather forecast** 気象［天気］予報

□ **weather forecasting** 気象［天気］予報

□ **website** 名ウェブサイト

□ **weigh** 動重さが～ある

□ **weight** 名重さ

□ **welcoming** 形快適な，心地良い

Word List

□ **well-known** 形 よく知られた，有名な

□ **Wernher von Braun** ヴェルナー・フォン・ブラウン《工学者であり，ロケット技術開発の最初期における最重要指導者のひとり。1912–1977年》

□ **Western world** 西欧諸国

□ **wheeled** 形 車輪の付いた，車輪で動く

□ **where to** どこで～すべきか

□ **whether** 接 ～かどうか，～かまたは…，～であろうとなかろうと

□ **whisper** 動 ささやく，小声で話す

□ **white dwarf** 白色矮星《大部分が電子が縮退した物質によって構成されている恒星の残骸であり（縮退星），恒星が進化の終末期にとりうる形態の一つ》

□ **whole** 形 全体の，すべての

□ **wide** 副 広く，大きく開いて

□ **width** 名 幅，広さ

□ **with the aim of** ～を目的として，～のために

□ **within** 前 ①～の中［内］に，～の内部に ②～以内で，～を越えないで

□ **wonder** 動 ①不思議に思う，（～に）驚く ②（～かしらと）思う **wonder if** ～ではないかと思う 名 驚き（の念），不思議なもの

□ **wooden** 形 木製の，木でできた

□ **work on** ～で働く，～に取り組む

□ **world** 熟 **in the world** 世界で **world of** ～の世界

□ **World War II** 第二次世界大戦《1939年（昭和14年）9月1日から1945年（昭和20年）8月15日または9月2日まで約6年にわたって続いたドイツ・イタリア・日本などの日独伊三国同盟を中心とする枢軸国陣営と，イギリス・フランス・中華民国・アメリカ・ソビエト連邦などを中心とする連合国陣営との間で戦われた戦争》

□ **worth** 名 価値，値打ち **worth of** （～に）相当するだけ

X

□ **X-ray** 名 ①《しばしば-s》X線，レントゲン ②レントゲン写真［検査］

□ **X-ray telescope** X線望遠鏡《X線スペクトルで遠隔物体を観測するように設計された望遠鏡》

Y

□ **years** 熟 **for years** 何年も

□ **yellow dwarf** 黄色矮星《太陽を含む，G型主系列星の別名》

□ **Yuri Gagarin** ユーリイ・ガガーリン《ソビエト連邦の軍人，パイロット，宇宙飛行士。人類初の有人宇宙飛行としてボストーク1号に単身搭乗した。1934–1968年》

Z

□ **Zhurong** 名 祝融号《マーズ・ローバーであり，中国が最初に地球以外の惑星に上陸させた探査車。中国国家航天局（CNSA）が火星に向けて打ち上げた天問1号の一部》

□ **zoom** 動 急速に動く **zoom around** あちこちに急速に動く

English Conversational Ability Test
国際英語会話能力検定

● E-CATとは…
英語が話せるようになるための
テストです。インターネット
ベースで、30分であなたの発
話力をチェックします。

www.ecatexam.com

● iTEP®とは…
世界各国の企業、政府機関、アメリカの大学
300校以上が、英語能力判定テストとして採用。
オンラインによる90分のテストで文法、リー
ディング、リスニング、ライティング、スピー
キングの5技能をスコア化。iTEP®は、留学、就
職、海外赴任などに必要な、世界に通用する英
語力を総合的に評価する画期的なテストです。

www.itepexamjapan.com

ラダーシリーズ

Amazing Space 宇宙のすべて

2023年12月2日　第1刷発行

著　者　エド・ジェイコブ

発行者　浦　晋亮

発行所　**IBCパブリッシング株式会社**
〒162-0804 東京都新宿区中里町29番3号
菱秀神楽坂ビル
Tel. 03-3513-4511　Fax. 03-3513-4512
www.ibcpub.co.jp

印刷　株式会社シナノパブリッシングプレス

装丁　伊藤 理恵　カバー写真 NASA

Printed in Japan
ISBN978-4-7946-0791-1